A Book Of

PRINCIPLES OF FINANCE

For
BBA (Semester - II)
As Per Pune University's Revised Syllabus
Effective from June 2013

Mrs. Meera Govindaraj
M.Com., M.B.A. (Finance)

NIRALI PRAKASHAN
Advancement of knowledge

N2913

PRINCIPLES OF FINANCE　　　　　　　　　　　　　　　**ISBN 978-93-83750-00-9**

First Edition : November 2013

© : **Author**

Published By :

NIRALI PRAKASHAN
Abhyudaya Pragati, 1312, Shivaji Nagar,
Off J.M. Road, PUNE – 411005
Tel - (020) 25512336/37/39, Fax - (020) 25511379
Email : niralipune@pragationline.com

Printed By :

Repro Knowledgecast Limited,
Thane

DISTRIBUTION CENTRES

PUNE

Nirali Prakashan
119, Budhwar Peth, Jogeshwari Mandir Lane
Pune 411002, Maharashtra
Tel : (020) 2445 2044, 66022708, Fax : (020) 2445 1538
Email : bookorder@pragationline.com

Nirali Prakashan
S. No. 28/27, Dhyari,
Near Pari Company, Pune 411041
Tel : (022) 24690371
Fax : (020) 24690316
Email : dhyari@pragationline.com
　　　　 bookorder@pragationline.com

MUMBAI

Nirali Prakashan
385, S.V.P. Road, Rasdhara Co-op. Hsg. Society Ltd.,
Girgaum, Mumbai 400004, Maharashtra
Tel : (022) 2385 6339 / 2386 9976, Fax : (022) 2386 9976
Email : niralimumbai@pragationline.com

DISTRIBUTION BRANCHES

NAGPUR

Pratibha Book Distributors
Above Maratha Mandir, Shop No. 3, First Floor,
Rani Jhanshi Square, Sitabuldi, Nagpur 440012,
Maharashtra, Tel : (0712) 254 7129

BENGALURU

Pragati Book House
House No. 1, Sanjeevappa Lane, Avenue Road Cross,
Opp. Rice Church, Bengaluru – 560002.
Tel : (080) 64513344, 64513355,
Mob : 9880582331, 9845021552
Email:bharatsavla@yahoo.com

JALGAON

Nirali Prakashan
34, V. V. Golani Market, Navi Peth, Jalgaon 425001,
Maharashtra, Tel : (0257) 222 0395
Mob : 94234 91860

KOLHAPUR

Nirali Prakashan
New Mahadvar Road,
Kedar Plaza, 1st Floor Opp. IDBI Bank
Kolhapur 416 012, Maharashtra. Mob : 9855046155

CHENNAI

Pragati Books
9/1, Montieth Road, Behind Taas Mahal, Egmore,
Chennai 600008 Tamil Nadu, Tel : (044) 6518 3535,
Mob : 94440 01782 / 98450 21552 / 98805 82331, Email : bharatsavla@yahoo.com

RETAIL OUTLETS

PUNE

Pragati Book Centre
157, Budhwar Peth, Opp. Ratan Talkies,
Pune 411002, Maharashtra
Tel : (020) 2445 8887 / 6602 2707, Fax : (020) 2445 8887

Pragati Book Centre
Amber Chamber, 28/A, Budhwar Peth,
Appa Balwant Chowk, Pune : 411002, Maharashtra,
Tel : (020) 20240335 / 66281669
Email : pbcpune@pragationline.com

Pragati Book Centre
676/B, Budhwar Peth, Opp. Jogeshwari Mandir,
Pune 411002, Maharashtra
Tel : (020) 6601 7784 / 6602 0855

PBC Book Sellers and Stationers
152, Budhwar Peth, Pune 411002, Maharashtra
Tel : (020) 2445 2254 / 6609 2463

MUMBAI

Pragati Book Corner
Indira Niwas, 111 - A, Bhavani Shankar Road, Dadar (W), Mumbai 400028, Maharashtra
Tel : (022) 2422 3526 / 6662 5254, Email : pbcmumbai@pragationline.com

www.pragationline.com　　　　　　　　　　　　　　　　　　　　info@pragationline.com

Preface ...

Finance is a branch of economics, a science that studies the management of funds (money and other assets). More specifically, through financial analysis, decisions and corrective actions can be taken regarding the collection and use of funds as to optimise their use toward the objectives of an organisation (states, companies and businesses) or individual.

Finance, involves the management, creation and study of money, banking, credit, investments, shares, capital markets, assets and liabilities, budgeting, forecasting, microfinance and mutual funds. Students become familiar with financial systems, which include the public, private and government spaces. They also study financial instruments related to countless assets and liabilities.

The objective of writing this book is to present the subject of 'Principles of Finance' strictly in accordance with the revised new 'Pune University Syllabus', for B.B.A. Semester-II. Every attempt has been made to present the matter in a simple and concise manner.

This book has been compiled by referring to various standard books on the subject.

I would take this opportunity to show my gratitude to my publishers Shri. Dinesh Bhai Furia and Shri. Jignesh Furia for the confidence reposed in me and for giving me this opportunity to reach out to the students of management studies.

The author would welcome feedback and suggestions for the improvement and development of the content. Although utmost care has been taken to keep the book error free, I take responsibility for any insufficiencies encountered. To err is human while to forgive is divine.

Any suggestions or comments towards the enhancement of the content of this book are most welcome at niralipune@pragationline.com.

Author

Syllabus ...

BBA (Sem. II : Course Code 203)

Unit 1: Introduction   (04 Lectures)
1.1   Finance – Definition – Nature and Scope of Finance Function.
1.2   Financial Management – Meaning – Approaches: Traditional, Modern.
1.3   Role of Finance Manager.

Unit 2: Sources of Finance   (16 Lectures)
2.1   External: Shares, Debentures, Public Deposits, Borrowing from banks: Meaning, Types, Advantages and Limitations of these sources.
2.2   Internal: Reserves and Surplus, Bonus shares, Retained earnings, Divided policy, Meaning, Advantages and Limitations of these sources.

Unit 3: Capital Structure   (14 Lectures)
3.1   Meaning – Criteria for determining capital structure
3.2   Factors affecting capital structure
3.3   Capitalisation – Meaning
3.4   Over capitalisation and Under capitalisation – Meaning, Causes, Consequences, Remedies

Unit 4: Financial Planning   (06 Lectures)
4.1   Meaning and Objectives
4.2   Process
4.3   Methods of Forecasting
4.4   Basic considerations
4.5   Limitations

Unit 5: Recent Trends in Business Finance   (08 Lectures)
Meaning and Nature of:
5.1   Venture Capital
5.2   Leasing
5.3   Microfinance
5.4   Mutal Fund

Contents ...

Chapter **1**...

Introduction

Contents ...

Learning Objectives:

- To understand the nature, importance and structure of finance related areas
- To know finance functions with other functions of a firm
- To understand the nature and scope of financial function
- To understand the different kinds of business organisations
- To become aware of financial management and understand the features, scope, and objectives of financial management
- To get acquainted with the organisational framework of financial management.

Introduction

Business is an organised entity, whose purpose is to sell goods and services to customers in order to earn profit for the owners. All the forms of business organisations undertake the following functions (by **Henry Fayol, the French Industrialist**):

1. Technical – related to production.
2. Commercial – involving buying, selling and exchange.
3. Financial activities – including such activities as search for capital and its optimum use.
4. Security – involving protection of property and person.
5. Accounting and
6. Managerial activities of planning, organisation, command co-ordination and control.

'Finance' as an activity and as a separate field of study is of recent origin. It was a branch of Economics till 1890.

1.1 Definitions

The term 'finance' has been defined in the following ways:

1. *"The practice of manipulating and managing money".*
   – Oxford Dictionary of Business and Management
2. *"Finance may be defined as the art and science of managing money".*
   – Khan and Jain
3. *"In general, Finance may be defined as the provision of money at the time it is wanted".*
   – S. N. Maheshwari
4. *"Finance is the money resources of a state, company, or a person".*
   – Oxford Dictionary

From the definitions stated above, we can say that Finance is that part of money resource of an individual, business or government, which is available for investment. Thus, when money is used to obtain more money, it is called finance. Expenditure incurred for consumption purposes is not finance.

Individuals save money to invest in various financial products made available by business firms such as shares and bonds, by government and by other agencies like Banks, Insurance companies, Stock markets etc. The objective is to earn income on investment.

Business firms require money to obtain manufacturing and other facilities, so as to produce goods and services. The finance for the same may come from the owner's savings or from lending agencies like banks, financial institutions etc.

Government needs finance to undertake various public welfare projects like – construction of dams, roads, railways for poverty alleviation programmes etc. Government may depend partly on its revenue from tax collections and may partly depend on public debts (i.e. borrowing from the people of the country).

Thus, Finance is inherent in all economic activities. In order to have a better understanding of the term 'Finance' it may be compared with money and funds.

1.1.1 Money Vs. Finance

The word money is derived from the Latin word *'moneta'* which was one of the names of 'Juno' the roman Goddess whose temple was used as a mint.

Money is an instrument that serves as a medium of exchange, has a standard of value and is a means to save or store purchasing power. Supply of money is the monopoly of the government of the country. In India, coins are minted by the Department of Finance and currency notes are issued by the Reserve Bank of India.

Money is used in business to get money. Finance is the activity which makes it possible. Thus, finance means arranging for money and utilising it for the stated purpose.

1.1.2 Funds Vs. Finance

Fund is a separate pool of monetary and other resources used to support designated activity, for e.g. Workmen Compensation Fund, Provident Fund etc. According to the International Accounting Standard No. 1, *"The term fund generally refers to cash and cash equivalents or to working capital"*. Working Capital Fund may mean Gross Working Capital or Net Working Capital. Gross Working Capital is the total amount invested in the Current Assets of the firm such as – Receivables, Cash, Bank Balances, Stock of Goods, Short-term Investment etc. whereas Net Working Capital means the excess of Current Assets over Current Liabilities. Current Liabilities are short-term obligations of the firm and includes Creditors, Bills Payable, Bank Overdraft etc. Net Working Capital indicates that part of the Current Asset which has been financed out of long-term liabilities of the business.

1.1.3 Finance and Related Disciplines

Finance as a separate field of study draws its concepts, principles, techniques and data from other disciplines – such as economics, accounting, marketing, production and quantitative methods.

The relationships of Finance with other disciplines is discussed below:

(A) Finance and Economics:

Economics is the science of production and distribution of wealth. The two branches of Economics are:

1. Micro-economics.
2. Macro-economics.

1. Micro-economics deals with the economic decisions of individual consumers, individual firms or producers. It explains the theories of maximising consumer satisfaction with the limited resources possessed. The 'Production Laws' aim at maximising cost or in other words, optimal use of productive resources. Micro-economics makes use of marginal analysis to explain laws of production and consumption.

The same marginal analysis is made use of in financial analysis as well. This can be explained with the help of an example:

Suppose, a firm has to decide between two alternatives – whether to continue with the existing machine or to replace the existing machine with a better one. For this purpose the incremental revenue expected from the replacement of the machine would be compared with the incremental cost of replacement of the asset. Suppose the new machine requires a cash outlay of ₹ 10,00,000 and existing machine could be sold for ₹ 2,50,000. That means the incremental outlay is only ₹ 7,50,000, (₹ 10,00,000 – ₹ 2,50,000) and not ₹ 10,00,000. In the same way, the expected revenue from the new machine would be compared with the revenue earned from the existing machine. Suppose, the revenue expected from the new machine is expected to be ₹ 12,00,000 whereas the benefits from the existing machine is ₹ 4,00,000. The incremental revenue will be ₹ 8,00,000. The comparison between the incremental revenue and incremental cost would help the financial executive to take a decision about replacement or otherwise of the machine.

2. Macro-economics is that branch of economics which deals in aggregates. It includes macro concepts such as – national income, general price-level, national output, money-market functioning of capital market, development and growth of an economy. Every firm operates in the overall macro-economic environment. The money policies of the government influence the cost of borrowing, and availability of funds. On the other hand, fiscal policies affect the availability of profits of the owner (after payment of tax and the pricing of the products or services).

(B) Finance and Accounting:

Finance draws its data from 'Accounting'. Accounting provides the needed input to the finance function. Accounting results in preparation of financial statements such as:

(i) Income Statement and

(ii) Position Statement

The financial statements are analysed with the help of techniques of analysis such as – ratio analysis, funds flow statement, trend analysis, comparative and common size statement which help interpret past performance. These analysis helps a finance manager in deciding about the future course of action.

'Finance' and 'Accounting' can be **differentiated** on the following grounds:

1. Accounting follows accrual system of recording, which means a revenue is recognised when sale is made or when the required services have already been rendered, irrespective of whether it is collected or not. Similarly, expenditure is recorded when it becomes due for payment and not when it is paid. This concept is used for arriving at the true profit or loss of the business. The profit may not be an indication of equivalent amount of cash within the firm. A firm might have earned profit but may fall short of funds, even to meet its day-to-day obligations, or may find it difficult to distribute the profit in the form of cash dividends to its owners.

Finance on the other hand considers the cash inflows and outflows. Revenue is recognised only when received in cash and expenses are recognised on actual payment of expenditure.

2. Accounting is concerned with recording what has happened in the past, whereas finance is concerned with the future. It involves decision-making under imperfect information and uncertainty. Hence, financial data is not as accurate as accounting data.

3. Accounting aims at arriving at accurate results of operations and in revealing the financial position of the business. On the other hand finance aims at maximising the wealth of the owners.

4. Finance aims at optimum use of funds whereas accounting aims at recording the monetary transactions. Accounting doesn't judge whether an expenditure should have been incurred or not.

1.2 Finance Function

Finance function may be defined as the procurement of the needed funds and their effective utilisation. There are two sides to the finance function:

1. Acquisition of the funds for the purposes of investment in various real assets of the firm. A firm can acquire funds from two sources:

   (i)   Ownership funds

   (ii) Borrowed funds

   Unincorporated firms like the sole proprietorship and partnership business, contribute capital from their personal savings as in the case with the sole proprietorship and partnership business. In case of Joint Stock Company, 'financial assets' or 'securities' such as shares and debentures are sold to investors in the capital markets to raise the needed funds. Firms can also borrow money from Banks, Financial institutions and other sources. Ownership funds comes with the expectation of profits or dividends whereas for the borrowed funds, a firm has to pay interest on the borrowings. Both the sources of funds involve cost. Cost is one of the important considerations while deciding about the financial mix.

2. The funds of a firm are used to purchase various real assets. Real assets can be tangible or intangible. Plant, Machinery, Furniture, Building, Inventory are tangible assets, whereas Patents, Copyrights, Technical know-how etc. are intangible assets. While choosing the alternative investments, the expected returns are to be considered.

It can be observed that the two aspects of finance function is related to the two sides of a Balance Sheet of a Firm, viz. Assets and Liabilities, as shown below:

Balance Sheet

Liabilities	Amount (₹)	Assets	Amount (₹)
Share Capital	....	Fixed Assets	....
Reserves and Surplus	....	Investment	....
Secured Loans	....	Current Assets	....
Current Liabilities and		Loans and Advances	....
Provisions	....	Miscellaneous Expenses	....
	....		....

The Liability side of the Balance Sheet indicates the sources of finance and the Asset side of the Balance Sheet represents the usage of the funds acquired.

1.2.1 Relationship of Finance Function with Other Functions of a Firm

Finance is an all pervasive activity of a business. All business activities are related to finance. It can be explained with the help of the following examples:

1. Recruitment and promotion of employees in the organisation is the responsibility of the personnel department, but the decision regarding the pay and incentive to be paid, is a finance function.

2. Sales promotion and advertisements are marketing functions but these activities require cash and hence affect the financial resources of the firm.

3. Decisions such as credit period to be allowed to credit customers, quantity of inventory to be maintained in the firm, are finance functions.

1.3 Nature and Scope of Finance Function

Nature of finance function has changed over the years since its emergence as a separate field of study. The nature of finance function can be studied under the following heads:

1. **Multidisciplinary:** Finance function is multidisciplinary in the sense that it draws knowledge, techniques and tools of analysis from various other disciplines, such as Economics, Accounting, Marketing, Production and Quantitative methods. Macro-economics provides knowledge of the macro-economic environment in which a firm is operating and the micro-economic environment provides, decision-making techniques. For example, the key-macro economic factors like growth rate of economy, the tax policy of the government, the foreign trade relations, the rate of inflation, the real rates of interests, etc. are used in deciding financial matters such as, what should the period and the amount of borrowings be the rate of discounting to

find the present value of future cash flows etc. The key to micro-economic theories – marginal analysis is used in taking various financial decisions. e.g. marginal utility, marginal product, etc.

2. **Lack of Unanimity:** The subject of finance is still in the process of development. There are still certain areas where controversies exist and for which no unanimous solutions have been reached as yet. 'Cost of capital' is still a disputed topic of 'finance'. The financial experts advocate conflicting opinions as to the way in which cost of capital can be measured.

3. **It is a Science as well as an Art:** Science is a body of knowledge, which has universal application, has accuracy and the scientific theories are based on systematic observation and experiment of a phenomena.

   On the other hand, art is a human creative skill. Finance function uses scientific methods of observation and experiment. It consists of certain basic principles and procedures based on various theories developed by experts in the field viz. cost of capital theories, capital structure etc. It also makes use of various statistical techniques, econometric models, for taking various financial decisions like – capital budgeting decisions, investment decisions, capital structure decisions etc. Thus, financial management is an applied science.

   Finance decisions cannot be wholly based on theories of finance. A financial manager has to use his discretion and judgement. Experience helps a finance manager in applying the theory or modifying the theory to suit the needs of the organisation.

   Thus, we can say Finance is both an art as well as a science.

4. **Finance Function as a Profession:** 'Finance' is the economical procurement of finance and its optimum utilisation. 'Finance' can be understood from another point of view. It refers to the consultation services provided by financial experts, to individual, firms or the government regarding managing the finance, making investments in the various, financial products like shares, bonds etc.

5. **All Pervasive in Nature:** Finance function is inherent in every function of an organisation. Starting from purchase, to production, to sale, to dividend distribution, finance function is involved. Literally every decision taken by a firm has financial implications. Thus, finance is an all pervasive function.

6. **Value of Money:** Finance is all related to money. Money although initially was considered as a standard measure of value and store of value, this is not true. Money, today is more valuable than money at a future date. In order to take effective decisions, the future flows are discounted at an appropriate rate, to know the present value of cash flows.

7. **Finance Function dependent on Economic Variables:** Finance decisions are affected by the inflation rates, monetary and fiscal (taxation etc.) policies of the government, banking regulation, business legislations etc.

1.4 Forms of Business Organisations

Finance function of a firm depends on the form of business organisation. On the basis of ownership and management, the following can be forms in which a business can be organised:

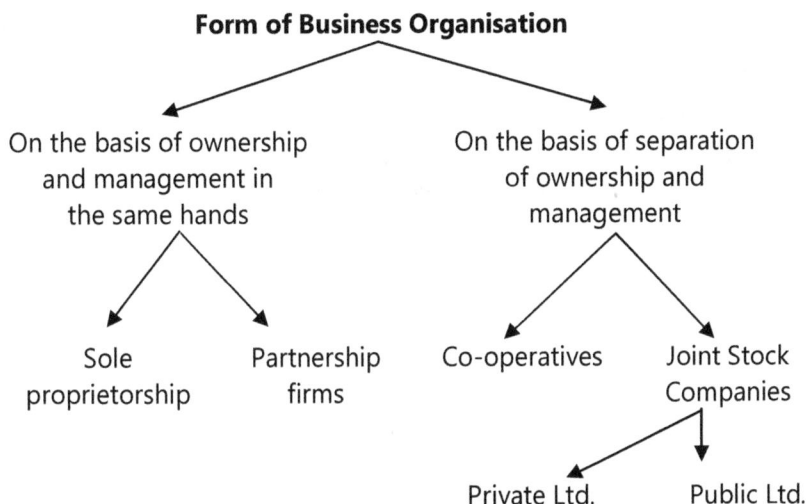

Form of Business Organisation

On the basis of ownership and management in the same hands → Sole proprietorship, Partnership firms

On the basis of separation of ownership and management → Co-operatives, Joint Stock Companies → Private Ltd., Public Ltd.

Fig. 1.1: Forms of Business Organisations

1.4.1 Sole Proprietorship

It is an unincorporated business owned by a single person, who contributes money and money's worth into the business, takes all the decisions, manages the whole business, enjoys all the profits and bears all the losses. The profits of the business is taxed at the proprietor's individual tax rate. The sole trader is personally liable for all the debts of the business. His personal property is also held liable for the liabilities of the business.

The capital of the sole proprietorship is limited to the personal wealth of the owner. The owner can borrow money in case of need. But, due to unlimited liability, the owner's capacity to borrow is restricted. Hence, such business firms remain small in size and cannot grow beyond a certain limit.

1.4.2 Partnership

It is an extension of sole proprietorship. This is a form of business owned and managed by two or more persons (minimum of 10 owners in case of Banking business and 20 in case of other businesses). The business comes into existence with the execution of a partnership deed (written agreement between the partners). The owners are called partners who share profits and losses of business in the agreed ratio. The partnership deed specifies the rights and duties of the partners. In India, partnership firms are governed by the *Indian Partnership Act* of 1932. The legislation regulates the relationship between partners themselves and also between partners and the outsiders.

Partnership enjoys a better capital base and better management, but suffers from the same limitations as a sole proprietorship i.e. unlimited liability of partners. Partner's liability is joint as well as several. Partners are jointly as well as individually liable to the creditors. Further, the capacity of partners to contribute capital is limited. Hence, it cannot grow beyond a certain limit. Finance function of these organisations is not very much complicated due to the small size on hand and ownership and management being vested in the same hands.

1.4.3 Co-operative Society

"A co-operative society is an organisation which has as its objectives, the promotion of economic interest of its members in accordance with co-operative principles". These societies were initially meant for economically weaker sections of the society, like agriculturalists, factory workers etc. who pooled their resources to gain from economies of large scale – especially agriculturalists. There can be consumer co-operatives, credit co-operatives, agricultural co-operatives etc. The management of the co-operatives is usually vested in a committee of members elected by the members on the basis of 'one man one vote' system. The co-operatives are meant to help the members.

The co-operatives come into existence through registration. The liability of the members is limited. These societies suffer from paucity of funds as the members are from a poor economic background. But, these societies may get grants and financial assistance by the government.

1.4.4 Joint Stock Company

A Joint Stock Company is a corporate enterprise that has a legal identity separate from that of its members. Most of the large businesses are organised in line with joint stock form. The salient features of a company are as follows:

1. Company is a legal person, separate from its members. A company can own assets, incur liability, enter into contracts, sue and be sued on its own name. A common seal is used as a signature of the company.

2. The liability of the shareholder is limited. They cannot be asked to pay beyond the issue price on the shares held by them. The private properties of the shareholder is not held liable for clearing the liabilities of the business.

3. In case of a private limited company, the number of members can go upto 50 (minimum being two), with restriction on the transfer of shares and the company is prohibited from issuing its shares to the public. A Public Ltd. Company must have a minimum of 7 members and the maximum number of members is unlimited. These companies allow their members to sell their shares at the stock exchange and can enjoy capital gain.

Public Ltd. companies are the most appropriate form of business for large firms. The reasons for this are as given below:

1. The risk to the investors is limited.
2. The company can grow due to availability of funds.
3. The investors enjoy liquidity due to free transferability of shares.

1.5 Financial Management

Financial management is concerned with effective management of finance of a firm. It is a managerial activity concerned with planning and controlling of the firm's financial resources. The term financial management has been defined as follows:

Definitions:

1. **Solomon** defines, *"Financial management is concerned with the efficient use of important economic resources namely capital funds".*

2. According to the **Oxford Dictionary,** *"The actions of the management of an organisation taken to ensure that the costs incurred and revenue are at acceptable levels. Financial control is assisted by the provision of financial information to management, by accountant and by the use of such techniques as Budgetary control and Standard costing, which highlight and analyse any variance".*

3. **Phillipatus** defines, *"Financial management is concerned with the managerial decisions that result in the acquisition and financing of long-term and short-term credits for the firm. As such it deals with the situations that require selection of specific assets (or combination of assets). The selection of specific liability (or combination of liabilities) as well as the problem of size and growth of an enterprise. The analysis of these decisions is based on the expected inflows and outflows of funds and their effects upon managerial objectives".*

4. **Guthaman and Dougall** say, *"Business Finance broadly can be defined as the activity concerned with planning, raising, controlling and administering of the funds used in the business".*

5. **Wheeler** defines, *"Business Finance is that business activity which is concerned with the acquisition and conservation of capital funds in meeting financial needs and overall objectives of a business enterprise".*

1.6 Features of Financial Management

From the definitions stated above the following features of financial management can be drawn:

1. **Managerial Activity:** Financial management is a managerial activity, hence involves managerial functions of planning, organising, directing, co-ordinating and controlling finance.

2. **Investment:** Investment is a part of financial management. Requirement of investment in plant, machinery or other assets can be taken as the starting point of all finance functions.

3. **Cost vs. Revenues:** This managerial activity ensures that the costs incurred while acquiring finance is minimum and revenue generated justifies the costs and inconvenience involved in acquiring capital.

4. **Size and Growth:** Financial management is concerned with answering questions such as:

   (a) How large an enterprise can be; and

   (b) How fast should it grow?

   It means even if a company's results are good, financial management would help management deal with the issue of growth.

5. **Forms of Assets:** Financial management is concerned with the decisions regarding the forms in which assets can be kept, i.e. the right mix of Fixed Assets and Current Assets.

6. **Combination of Liabilities:** Decision regarding combination of liability means decision regarding the Debt-equity ratio i.e. the proportion of borrowed funds to owner's funds. These decisions are called as capital structure decisions.

7. **Profit Planning:** In order to optimise the investment decisions and financial decisions, profit planning must be done. Profit planning helps to anticipate the relationship between cost i.e. variable and fixed cost, volume of sales and profit.

8. **Report to Management:** In order to control, the concerned persons are required to provide periodical reports to the management.

1.7 Scope and Approaches to Financial Management

The scope of financial management has been widening since its origin in 1890. It was a branch of economics then. Rapid industrialisation, technological innovations and inventions, intense competition, increasing participation of the government in economic affairs, globalisation etc. has widened the scope of financial management.

(I) Traditional Approach

In the beginning stages of development (1920-1940), financial management theories were applied for managing certain important events in the life of a firm viz.,

1. Promotion of a company i.e. setting-up of a company.

2. Reorganisation: Changes in the capital mix.

3. Expansion of firm.

4. Diversification of firm.

5. Acquisition and mergers.

The finance manager's duty was confined to determination of requirement of finance and sources of finance to raise the required funds.

Traditional approach evolved during 1920s and continued till 1940s.

It included the following activities:

(i) Arrangement of funds from financial institution.

(ii) Arrangement of funds through issue of financial instruments like shares, debentures, bonds etc.

(iii) Looking after the legal requirements with regard to these sources of arrangement of funds.

Thus traditional approach included only the arrangement of external sources of finance for the company. The functions of finance manager included:

(a) To keep accurate financial records;

(b) Prepare reports of performance and status of the company;

(c) To manage cash in a way to facilitate the timely payment of dues by the company.

Limitations of Traditional Approach

The traditional approach was criticised severely in the 1950s due to the following reasons:

(i) The approach restricted the scope of finance function to – raising of funds and its administration. The result of this was that the finance function included only study of the operation of the supplier of funds like banks, financial institution, investors etc. The internal financing through use of reserves and issue of bonus shares, the dividend decision etc. were not included in finance function.

(ii) According to the approach, finance manager was to make financial decisions only during such important and infrequent events such as mergers, incorporations, re-organisation of enterprises etc., day to finance decisions as to how many days of credit to be allowed to customers, whether to pay dividend or not and if yes how much, how much credit to be demanded from the supplier, the selection of best machinery for the firm, when to place order for the supply of stores and materials, whether to buy a part or to produce it, and so on.

(iii) The approach ignored the non-corporate enterprises such as single ownership concerns and partnership firms.

(iv) The approach did not give any importance to the allocation of funds to the various uses. It did not provide answers to the following questions as pointed out by Solomon:

- Should an enterprise commit capital funds to certain purpose?

- Do the expected returns meet financial standards of performance?

- How should these standards be set and what is the cost of capital funds to the enterprise?
- How does cost vary with the mixture of financing methods used?

The method ignored 'capital budgeting' and 'determination of cost of capital' from the purview of financial management.

(II) Modern Approach

At present the scope of financial management has shifted from raising funds on important occasions of promotion, expansion, diversification etc. to efficient and effective use of funds and to solving financial problems. The scope of Financial Management includes the following decisions:

1. Investment Decision
2. Financing Decision
3. Dividend Decision
4. Liquidity Decision

1. Investment Decision

A firm has to take a decision regarding the various assets to be acquired to achieve the plans of the organisation. The various assets required by a firm can be:

(a) Fixed Assets: These assets are purchased for long-term use, such as Plant and Machinery, Building, Furniture, Equipment etc. The amount of money invested in the Fixed Assets is called as Fixed Capital.

(b) Current Assets: These assets are meant for short-term use, such as Stock, Debtors, Cash and Bank Balances etc. The funds invested in these assets is called Working Capital.

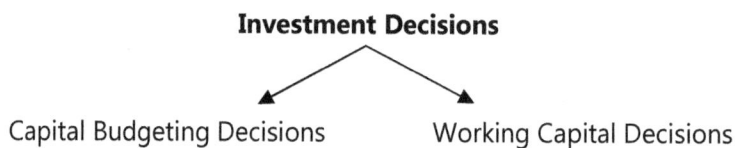

Investment Decisions

Capital Budgeting Decisions   Working Capital Decisions

(i) Capital Budgeting Decisions

Capital budgeting decisions involves commitment of funds to long-term assets of the company. Capital budgeting decisions have long-term impact, the funds involved are huge and these decisions are irreversible, hence a lot of caution is required while committing funds. Capital Budgeting decisions involve the determination of the profitability of the investment proposals. For this purpose, the following data is acquired:

(a) **Cash flows:** Both cash outflow and future expected cash inflow.

(b) Determination of a discounting rate for converting the future cash flows in terms of value of money. Normally, the required rate of return or the opportunity cost of capital is used for the purpose.

(c) Comparison of the discounted cash inflow and outflow to determine the appropriate investment plan. If the present value of cash inflow is more than the present value of cash outflow, the project may be accepted.

(ii) Working Capital

Working capital is required for the day-to-day management of the business organisation. It has two versions: Gross Working Capital and Net Working Capital. Gross Working Capital refers to the amount to be invested in Stocks, Debtors, Cash and Bank Balances etc. Net Working capital refers to the excess of Current Assets over Current Liabilities. A finance manager has to decide about the amount to be invested in the working capital so that production is not adversely affected. At the same time company should not have excess amount of funds blocked in these current assets. The decision about the stock of inventory to be maintained, the period of credit to be allowed to customers, the amount of overdraft facilities to be availed of etc., are part of working capital decision. If large amounts are blocked in the current assets, the company would lose opportunities of productive investment and at the same time the cost will increase, causing a decline in the profitability.

2. Financing Decisions

Finance decision is the second important function to be performed by the financial manager. The source of raising finance and the timing of finance, for the investment needs of the firm must be determined. The decision about the financing mix is called the capital structure decisions. An optimum mix of debt and owned funds has to be decided in such a way that the cost of raising finance is minimised and market value of the firm is maximised.

Use of debt in the capital structure increases the return to the shareholders but excess of debt may be considered risks by both the shareholders as well as the lenders of finance. The company may run the risk of insolvency i.e. incapability to meet business obligations. On the other hand, excessive use of owned funds may not give good returns to the shareholders resulting in reduction of share prices and low market value of the firm.

Risk is one of the considerations. In practice, the firm has to consider many other factors such as control, flexibility, loan convenants, legal aspects etc. in deciding capital structure.

3. Dividend Decision

It is the third major decision of financial management. Dividend decision involves the decision regarding the division of profit into 'dividend' and 'retained earnings'. Dividend, here refers to the distribution of profits earned, to the shareholders, in the form of cash. Payment of cash dividend may have long-term implications. It reduces the cash reserves on one hand and the profits on the other. In other words, it affects the short-term liquidity of the company and long-term growth plans. Retained earnings are the profits which are not distributed to partners but are kept for future expansion and growth of the enterprise. Retained earnings provide internal sources of finance. There is no cost involved in using the profits of the firm.

But non-payment of dividend may affect the sentiments in the capital market and may affect the share prices adversely. Hence, dividend payment decision should be a trade off between cash dividend and retained earnings.

1.8 Objectives of Financial Management

Objectives guide the management towards effective decision-making. All functions of management viz. planning, organising, staffing, directing and controlling have to be goal oriented. As is the case with general management, financial management decisions must also have definite goals.

The alternative goals that can be pursued by a financial manager, can be:

1. Maximisation of profit;
2. Maximisation of earning per share or Maximisation of return on equity;
3. Wealth maximisation.

1. Maximisation of Profit

Profit is the excess of revenue over costs. It may mean gross profit, net profit, profit before tax or profit after tax, it may be profit available to the equity shareholders after payment of tax and preference dividend.

Profit is the natural objective of an organisation. The profit approach to financial management implies that the major financial decisions viz. investment decisions, financing decisions and dividend policy decisions of a firm should be oriented towards maximisation of profits. The **rationale behind** profit maximisation can be stated as follows:

(i)   Profit is required for the very survival of a firm.

(ii) It leads to allocation of resources of money, men and machine towards the most profitable activity.

(iii) It leads to overall economic welfare. Goods and services which do not generate profits, are not produced.

(iv) Profit can be maximised by producing maximum output out of a given input or by the use of minimum input for producing a desired quantity of output. This is possible only when funds are used efficiently.

Objectives of the Profit Maximisation Approach

Profit maximisation objective has been criticised on the following grounds:

1. Objective of profit maximisation ignores the welfare of the society. Undesirable goods and services may be produced.

2. Profit maximisation objective leads to unequal distribution of income and wealth.

3. This objective is in conflict with the objectives of other parties interest in the firm, such as customers, employees, government etc.

4. Profit is a vague term. Profit maximisation may mean maximisation of short-term profits, long-term profit, Earnings Before Interest and Taxes (EBIT), Profit After Tax (PAT), Total Profits or Earnings Per Share (EPS) etc. Profit maximisation is vague and impracticable.

5. This approach ignores the timing of return. Profits earned in two different periods cannot be compared without considering the time value of money. The profit maximisation approach cannot make use of discounting, since profit is not synonymous with cash earnings. A significant part of income (credit sales) might not be in a realised form and at the same time a part of expenditure might not represent cash outflow.

6. Profit maximisation may not always lead to enhanced earnings for the equity shareholders. The following illustration proves this:

    Suppose the company has 1,00,000 shares and EBIT (Earning After Tax) is ₹ 10,00,000. In order to increase the profit, the company makes an investment yielding a profit/income of 8%. Let us further suppose that the company financed the investment by issuing further 50,000 shares. The total earnings of the company after earning investment income would be 14,00,000. Profit has increased but the earning per share has come down from ₹ 10 $\left(\dfrac{₹\ 10,00,000}{1,00,000\ \text{shares}}\right)$ to ₹ 9.33

    (14,00,000 ÷ 1,50,000) per share.

    Thus, profit maximisation may not provide high earnings to the shareholders.

2. Maximisation of Earning Per Share (EPS)

Earning per share is calculated by dividing the profits left for ordinary shareholders i.e. profit after tax and preference dividend, is divided by the number of ordinary shares held by the members of the company.

Maximisation of Return on Equity:

$$\dfrac{\text{Profit available for equity shareholders}}{\text{Equity shareholders fund}} \times 100$$

EPS was seen as an important measure of performance in the 1950's and 1960's, but its significance has declined due to the following limitations:

1. It ignores the timing of profits as is the case with the profit maximisation approach. Firms might be paying in the present for the acquisition of production and other facilities but the returns might be generated after some time. There is time value attached to returns, which is not considered under the EPS maximisation approach as is the case with profit maxmisation.

2. It ignores the risk attached to expected benefits. There is uncertainty associated with further profits which is not considered, under the profit maximisation approach.

3. In order to increase EPS, firms might not make dividend payments, thereby retaining profits as a source of cheap finance. Such a dividend policy may not be to the advantage of the shareholders.

3. Wealth Maximisation

Wealth means riches. It is created when cash inflows from a financial activity is more than the cash outflow. For example, in case of households, wealth is said to have increased when valuable properties like land, investments etc. are bought. The purchase can be made out of the savings of the individual or can be bought by borrowing. In the latter case, wealth is created only when the expected inflow of money is more than the cash outflows.

Wealth in the context of a business means – maximisation of the value of a firm. The wealth maximisation approach to financial management means:

1. Increasing the value of a firm.

2. Increase in the market value per share.

3. Every financial decision generates net present value.

When cash inflow generated by an income generating asset is more than the cash outflow; the difference is a value addition to the value of assets available with the business. Thus, there is an increase in the wealth of the firm.

In order to maximise wealth, the finance manager will have to compare the cash outflow with the future expected cash inflow. An important aspect of such a comparison is the timing of the cash flow. Both the cash outflow and cash inflow may not take place in the same year. Cash outflow might be in the beginning and cash inflows might be generated in the future years. Value of money is related to time. Money received today is more valuable than that received in the future years. This is called Time value of money.

In order to obtain the present value of the future cash flows an appropriate discounting rate is used, called as hurdle rate, cut-off rate etc. This rate is determined keeping in view the opportunities available for investment, the expectation of returns of the shareholders/owners. If shareholders expect a return of 10% on the investment and company decides to take this as the discounting rate, then the present value of future cash flows will be calculated as follows:

Years	Cash flows	Present value factor @ 10%	Present value
0	(1,00,000)	1	(1,00,000)
1	30,000	0.909	27,270
2	30,000	0.81	24,300
3	32,000	0.729	23,328
4	22,000	0.656	14,4332
5	35,000	0.591	20,685
	1,35,000	**Total**	**1,10,015**

Net Present Value = Present value of cash inflow – Present value of cash outflow

$$= 1,10,015 - 1,00,000$$

$$= 10,015$$

The addition to wealth of the firm is ₹ 10,015.

It can be observed that a financial action which has a positive net present value creates wealth and if the criteria is followed in all financial decisions, the wealth will be maximised. Wealth maximisation is by far the most appropriate goal of financial management due to the following reasons:

1. This approach takes care of the timing of returns. Both cash outflow and cash inflows are discounted with the 'hurdle rate' which is the minimum rate of return that must be met for a company to undertake a particular project.

2. It takes care of the risk involved in the estimation of future cash flows. The discount rate is adjusted to consider the risk of uncertainty. Higher the risk higher is the discounting factor.

3. Wealth maxmisation leads to that course of action which generates the highest net present value. It automatically takes care of the interests of other interested parties, besides increasing the value of the firm. An increase in the value of the firm leads to the increase in the market price of the shares. Increase in the share price is the indicator of the overall performance of the firm.

Limitations of the Approach

This objective of financial management is acceptable as shareholders are the owners of a company. Since they provide risk loss capital to the company, their interest must get priority and must be protected. But it suffers from the following limitations:

1. If the shares of the firm are not quoted in the market, it would be difficult to measure the value of shares. The best way then would be to take the EPS. If EPS is increasing constantly and the intrinsic value of the shares is high, it can be concluded that the wealth of the shareholder is growing.

2. Share prices are dependent on several factors. Performance of a firm is one of the factor. Market price of the share is influenced by economic and political conditions prevailing in the country, speculative transactions etc.

3. In spite of the above limitations, wealth maximisation is considered as the best objective of financial management.

1.9 Organisational Framework of Financial Management

1.9.1 Introduction

Financial decisions are vital and are continuous in nature. Hence, these functions must be organised effectively. *'Organising is the process of dividing the work into convenient tasks or duties, grouping of such duties in the form of positions, grouping of various positions into departments and sections, assigning duties to individual positions and delegating authority to each position so that the work is carried on as planned".*

Most of the large firms place the finance functions in the hands of the top management consisting of Board of Directors, Chief Executive and Chairman. The reasons being:

1. Financial decisions are crucial for the survival, growth and development of a firm.

2. Financial decisions determine the solvency of the firms meaning the firms ability to pay its debts when it falls due for payment.

3. Centralised finance function can result in a number of economies to the firm like experts in the field can be made available, finance can be raised centrally at minimum possible cost etc.

1.9.2 Organisation

The organisation of the department of finance will differ from organisation to organisation. It is determined by such factors as size of the firm, nature of business, capabilities of finance personnel, financing operations, etc. Besides the designation of financial officer also differs from firm to firm. In some cases 'Finance Manager' is the head of the finance department and in others Vice-President Finance, Director of Finance or Financial controller may be the finance department's top executives.

The functions of finance can be conveniently divided into two groups. The group head may be preferring the functions of a Treasurer or a controller. Treasurer is a person who is responsible for looking after the money and other assets of the organisation. This may include overseeing the provision of the organisation's finances as well as some control over the way money is spent. The chief accounting executive is called controller in the USA. The controller is normally concerned with financial reporting, taxation and auditing. In India the designation of 'Treasurer' and 'Controller' is not common. The jobs of both may be handed over to the same 'Finance Manager' i.e. in case of small companies and may be handed over to two different managers.

The organisational chart of a big organisation is given below:

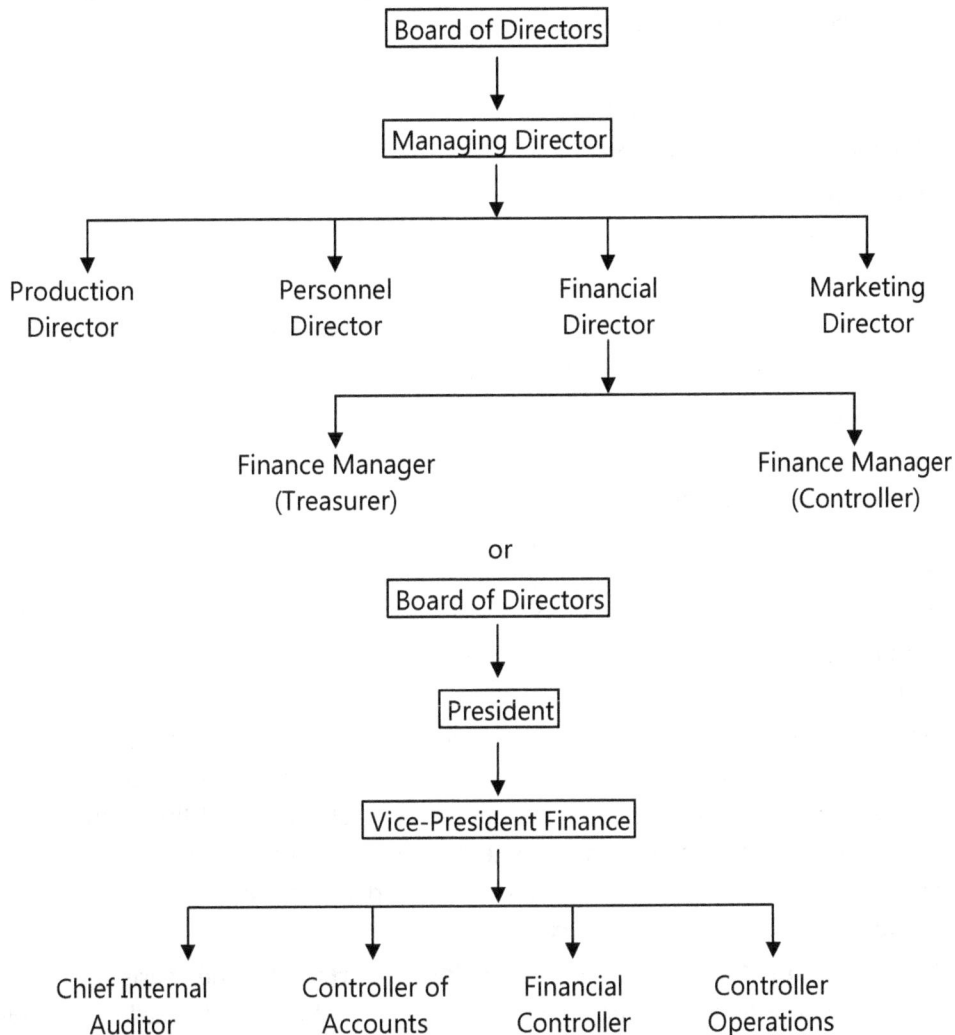

```
                        ┌──────────────────┐
                        │ Board of Directors│
                        └──────────────────┘
                                 │
                                 ▼
                        ┌──────────────────┐
                        │ Managing Director│
                        └──────────────────┘
                                 │
        ┌────────────────┬───────┴────────┬────────────────┐
        ▼                ▼                ▼                ▼
   Production        Personnel        Financial        Marketing
   Director          Director         Director         Director
                                          │
                          ┌───────────────┴───────────────┐
                          ▼                               ▼
                   Finance Manager                 Finance Manager
                    (Treasurer)                     (Controller)
```

or

```
                        ┌──────────────────┐
                        │ Board of Directors│
                        └──────────────────┘
                                 │
                                 ▼
                           ┌───────────┐
                           │ President │
                           └───────────┘
                                 │
                                 ▼
                    ┌──────────────────────┐
                    │ Vice-President Finance│
                    └──────────────────────┘
                                 │
        ┌────────────────┬───────┴────────┬────────────────┐
        ▼                ▼                ▼                ▼
  Chief Internal    Controller of     Financial        Controller
  Auditor           Accounts          Controller       Operations
```

The various finance functions can be grouped into two categories, irrespective of whether the designation are that of Treasurer and Controller or not.

1.9.3 Functions of Treasurer

The main function of the treasurer is to manage the firm's funds. His major duties include:

   (i)   Forecasting the financial needs,
   (ii) Administering the flow of cash,
   (iii) Managing credit,
   (iv) Floating securities,
   (v)   Maintaining relations with financial institutions and
   (vi) Protecting the funds and securities.

1.9.4 Functions of Controller

The functions of a controller include:

(i)   Providing information to formulate accounting and costing policies,

(ii)   Preparation of financial reports,

(iii) Direction of internal auditing,

(iv) Budgeting,

(v)   Inventory control, taxes etc.

In India, "Financial Manager" designation is more popular. Some of the functions of the controller is performed by company secretaries. The main function of a financial manager is the management of company's funds. The financial duties are often combined with others.

1.9.5 Role of a Finance Manager

A finance manager is the person responsible for carrying out finance functions. A finance manager occupies a key position in the modern enterprise. The role of finance manager is becoming more and more pervasive, intensive and significant in solving the complex management problems of today's business organisations. The functions of a finance manager is not confined to record-keeping, preparation of financial reports, raising of funds when needed etc. He is involved in the most vital decisions of allocation of capital. His main functions include:

1. **Financial forecasting:** Financial forecasting is the technique of determining in advance the requirement and utilisation of funds for a future period. It is a plan based on the sales forecast. It states the amount of funds and the timing of funds requirement. For the purpose various techniques are used such as- percentage sales method and regression method. Both the Fixed capital requirement and working capital requirement must be forecasted.

2. **Planning and Preparation of Financial Reports:** On the basis of financial forecasting the finance manager may prepare a profit plan also called as budget. Proforma Profit and loss account, proforma Balance sheet, Cash and funds flow statements and various ratios.

3. **Raising of Funds:** A finance manager must know the various sources of raising funds. He must know **the capital market** thoroughly. He must keep himself aware of the latest trends in financing so that he can use those for the organisation whenever conventional methods fail. Every source of funds has its own suitability. Finance manager must analyse the various sources of funds and choose the best one. Due to globalisation, corporate enterprises can now raise funds from the foreign markets. Foreign institutional investors and NRIs can also be approached for funds.

Raising funds involves lot of **formalities**. Finance manager must be aware of the various legislations and rules that affect the raising of funds through a particular source. These may include a resolution by the board, special resolution by shareholders, permission of government and company law board and so on.

While selecting a particular source of funds, he should keep in mind the changes it may cause to the **capital structure** of the company. Such change must be approved by the board and company. A change in the capital structure can change the cost of capital, can change the value of the firm, and can also cause the 'earning per share' (EPS) to change. He should study the impact of every source of fund thoroughly.

Besides, the 'cost benefit analysis' of the source is of top most importance. The aim should be to bring down the overall cost of capital of the company.

4. **Allocation of Funds:** The funds of the organisation need to be utilised efficiently. The funds of the company are used to buy fixed assets, to meet working capital requirements, to pay dividends to the shareholders, to repay debt, to make investment in securities of other companies, govt., and other institution etc. Finance manager takes decisions regarding the allocation of funds for all these uses so as to optimise the benefits. For instance he may have to find out whether current assets should be used to finance a particular fixed asset or a long term source of funds such as loan, issue of shares, leasing etc, should be used, whether liquid assets of the company should be used to pay dividend or overdraft facility should be availed.

Points to Remember

- **Finance** may be defined as the art and science of managing money.
- **Finance and related disciplines:**
  - (i) Finance and economics: Macro-economics and micro-economics
  - (ii) Finance and accounting
- **Nature and scope of financial functions:**
  - (i) Multidisciplinary
  - (ii) Lack of unanimity
  - (iii) It is a science as well as an art
  - (iv) Finance function as a profession
  - (v) All pervasive in nature
  - (vi) Value of money
  - (vii) Finance function dependent on economic variables
- **Forms of Business Organisations:**
  - (i) Sole Proprietorship
  - (ii) Partnership
  - (iii) Co-operative Society
  - (iv) Joint Stock company

- **Financial Management**: It is concerned with the efficient use of important economic resources namely capital funds.

- **Features of Financial Management:**
  (i)   Managerial Activity
  (ii)   Investment
  (iii) Cost vs. Revenues
  (iv) Size and Growth
  (v)   Forms of Assets
  (vi) Combination of liabilities
  (vii) Profit planning
  (viii) Report to management

- **Scope and Approaches to Financial Management:**
  (i)   Traditional Approach
  (ii)   Modern Approach

- **Objectives of Financial Management**
  (i)   Maximisation of Profit
  (ii)   Maximisation of Earning Per Share (EPS)
  (iii) Maximisation of return on equity
  (iv) Wealth Maximisation

Questions for Discussion

I.   State whether the following statements are True or False:

(i)   Traditionally the role of Finance Manager was restricted to raising of funds and allocation of funds.

(ii)   Wealth maximisation objective is the widely accepted objective of finance management.

(iii) The designation of Treasurer and Controller is popular in India.

(iv) Financing decision is also called capital structure decision.

(v)   Limited liability feature is one of the important features of company form of organisation.

(vi) Discounting factor helps in determining the timing of cash flows.

(vii) Profit maximisation approach considers the time value of money.

(viii) Finance means capital.

(ix) The funds invested in the current assets of a business is called gross working capital.

II. Choose the appropriate answer:

(i)   Finance refers to the _____

    (a) money available for transaction purposes

    (b) money kept to meet unforeseen contingencies

    (c) money kept to invest in the productive assets, with the object of earning more money

    (d) all of the above

(ii) The separate pool of monetary and other resources kept to support a stated activity is called _____

    (a) retained earnings

    (b) funds

    (c) reserves

    (d) working capital

(iii) Working capital is required _____

    (a) to finance the acquisition of fixed assets

    (b) to purchase securities of government

    (c) to carry out the day-to-day operations of the business

    (d) to acquire financial services for the working of the organisation

(iv) The amount invested in the Fixed Assets of the company is called _____

    (a) Fixed Capital

    (b) Net Working Capital

    (c) Permanent Capital

    (d) Reserve Capital

(v) EPS increases _____

    (a) when company's earnings after tax increases

    (b) when firm's earnings before tax increases

    (c) when the earning left after payment of preference dividend increases

    (d) when the earning kept as retained earnings increases

(vi) Increase in profits need not necessarily lead to _____

    (a) increase in share prices

    (b) increase in earnings per share

    (c) increase in the value of the firm

    (d) increase in the dividend pay-out

IV. Differentiate between:

(a) Finance and Accounting

(b) Finance and Funds

(c) Fixed Assets and Current Assets

(d) Limited Liability and Unlimited Liability

(e) Functions of Treasurer and Function of Controller

(f) Earning per share and Market price of shares

V. Write short notes on:

(a) Time-value of money

(b) Role of Finance Manager

(c) Finance is an art and a science

(d) Relationship of finance with Economics

(e) Agency conflict

(f) Risk-return trade off

VI. Questions:

1. Explain the wealth maximisation objective of Financial Management.

2. What is the scope of Financial Management?

3. Compare and contrast the wealth maximisation and profit maximisation objective of Financial Management.

4. How are the Financial Management functions organised in large firms?

5. Explain the limitations of profit maxmisation objectives of Financial Management.

6. Discuss the nature of Financial Function. How is it related to other functions of management?

Questions from Previous Pune University Examinations

1. Objectives of Financial Management.   **[April 2009]**

2. Explain concept of Financial Management with its scope and objectives. **[April 2009]**

3. Define Financial Management? Explain in detail the functions of Financial Management.   **[Oct. 2009]**

4. Objectives of Financial Management.   **[April 2010]**

5. Write short note on Role of Finance Manager.   **[Oct. 2010]**

6. Define 'Financial Management'. Also explain in detail its scope and objectives.

                                                [Oct. 2010]

7. Explain meaning of 'finance'. Also explain nature and scope of finance function.

                                                [Oct. 2010]

8. Role of Finance Manager.   **[April 2011]**
9. Scope of Finance Function.   **[April 2011]**
10. Objectives of Financial Management.   **[Oct. 2011]**
11. Define Finance Function. Explain in detail the nature and scope of Finance Function.
                                                                        [Oct. 2011]
12. Objectives of Financial Management.   **[April 2012]**
13. Role of Finance Manager.   **[Oct. 2012]**
14. Define Finance Management. Explain the scope and objectives of Financial Management.   **[Oct. 2012]**
15. Role of Finance Manager.   **[April 2013]**
16. Define Financial Management. Explain scope and objectives of Financial Management.   **[April 2013]**

■■■

Chapter 2...

Sources of Finance

Contents ...

Learning Objectives:

- To understand the external sources of finance
- To get acquainted with shares, debentures, public deposits, borrowings from banks, term loans, bridge financing and loan syndication
- To know the internal sources of finance
- To understand the role of depreciation
- To study the merits and demerits of internal sources of finance.

Introduction

A company can raise finance through any of the Sources of Finance available. Every source of finance has its own merits and demerits. A company keeps in view its own requirements, while choosing a particular source of finance.

2.1 Factors Determining the Choice of a Source of Finance

The various factors to be considered while choosing a source of finance are discussed below:

1. **Period of Finance**

   Finance may be needed for a short-period of time i.e. upto one year, or may be required for a longer period of time i.e. between 1 year and 5 years, or may be required for a still longer period of time i.e. beyond 5 years period.

   Normally working capital is required for a short period, e.g. payment of wage bill. Bank overdraft, Discounting of Bills can be a good source of finance. For purchasing Fixed Assets long-period of sources of finance may be tapped, e.g. issue of share, long-term loans from Banks and Financial institutions.

2. **Cost of Funds**

   Cost is an important factor while determining the source of finance. Cost of funds includes the rate of interest payable, floatation cost or cost of raising finance through the said source, in case of issue of shares the expected dividend and EPS, the redemption value of tax benefit etc.

   A company does a catalyst analysis while selecting the best source of finance.

3. **Amount of Finance**

   Each source of finance has its own capacity to generate funds, e.g. issue of shares can generate large amounts of finance if the nominal value of share is small and company is profit-making. On the other hand, Trade Creditors, Bank Overdraft etc. have limited capacity to generate funds.

4. **Availability of Capital Markets**

   Accessibility to the specified source of finance is important while deciding the source of finance. A company which has already borrowed large amounts on term loan, may not be able to obtain further loans as the lender would find it risky. In such a situation, the company may have to turn to other sources of finance like ploughing back to profit, i.e. the use of unutilised profits of the company.

5. **Shareholders Expectations**

   Shareholders desire concerning 'control' of the company is an important consideration. Issue of further shares, when existing shareholders are incapable to use their preemptive rights, will lead to dilution of their controlling power. If shareholders wish to keep their power intact, then they may not support further issue. In such cases, other sources of finance have to be resorted to.

Besides, if shareholders prefer cash dividends to transfer of earnings to reserves, internal sources of financing may be difficult.

Directors will have to keep the needs and expectations of the shareholders in mind because they are in agency relationship with the owners.

6. **Trading on Equity**

   Use of debt capital, as the capital structure of a company, creates financial leverage. When company is earning high rates of return and the rate of interest on the debt capital is lower, the surplus return on the debt capital is enjoyed by the ordinary shareholders. The EPS increases. If a company is desirous of 'Trading on equity' i.e. enjoy the benefits of Financial Leverage, debt capital shall be included in the capital structure of the company.

7. **Risk**

   Risk here means risk of insolvency, i.e. incapability to meet the obligations of interest payment and repayment of the principle amount. If a company has not been enjoying sound liquidity position, it would be better to go in for issue of shares or internal finance methods instead of using long-term debts like issue of debentures, borrowing of term-loan etc. as then servicing the debt may become a burden.

8. **Government regulations**

   The monetary and fiscal policies of the Government and SEBI guidelines must be kept in view. For example, if the company decides to issue bonus shares out of retained profits, then the guidelines issued by the Securities and Exchange Board of India (SEBI) should be followed.

2.2 Sources of Finance

Sources of finance can be classified as follows:

(A) On the Basis of Period

Organisations need finance for both short period i.e. upto one year's time, as well as for long periods. On the basis of the periodicity there can be two sources of finance:

   (i)   **Long-term sources:** These sources provide uninterrupted supply of funds for a long-period. Company can use the funds for a long period and need not bother to repay it out of the current liquid assets. Normally, firms use long-term source for the purchase of fixed assets and to finance the permanent working capital needs. The long-term sources of finance include issue of shares and debentures and term loans etc.

(ii) Short-term sources: These sources of finance provide funds upto one year's time. Temporary working capital needs are financed out of short-term sources of finance. These funds are repayable within a period of one year. Advances from commercial banks, public deposits, trade creditors (i.e. delay in payment to suppliers), advance from customers etc. are examples of short-term sources of finance.

(B) On the Basis of Ownership

On the basis of ownership, the sources of finance can be grouped into two categories:

(i)   Owned funds
(ii)   Borrowed funds

(i)   Owned funds: These funds are provided by the owners of a firm. These include issue of equity shares, and preference shares and use of depreciation funds and undistributed profits i.e. retained earnings of the company.

(ii) Borrowed funds: These are provided by Banks, financial institutions, debenture holders and deposit holders. A company is under legal obligation to pay interest on these funds and to repay the principle amount after the stated period of time. A company is required to provide security of its assets to the lender. Such a charge may be a fixed charge or a floating charge.

(C) On the basis of the Sources of Generation of Finance

Finance may be generated from within the firm or from an external source. On the basis of the generation of finance, the two sources of finance can be:

(i)   External sources of funds: All the sources of funds, except reserves and depreciation funds, are external sources of funds. These include issue of shares, debentures, borrowing of loans, trade creditors etc. These sources involve various costs: opportunity cost, floatation cost and servicing costs etc.

(ii) Internal sources of funds: These funds are created by a firm out of its operational activities and take the form of reserves funds and depreciation funds. These sources do not involve any flotation cost, servicing costs etc. But the cost is measured in terms of expectations of the ordinary shareholders or the owners. If the use of reserves are expected to generate lower returns than what the owners could earn by investment elsewhere, then the firm must not use retained earnings for capitalisation, rather it should distribute it to the shareholders. Hence, the cost of utilisation of retained earnings is the expectation of the shareholders in terms of returns from investment.

2.3 External Sources of Finance

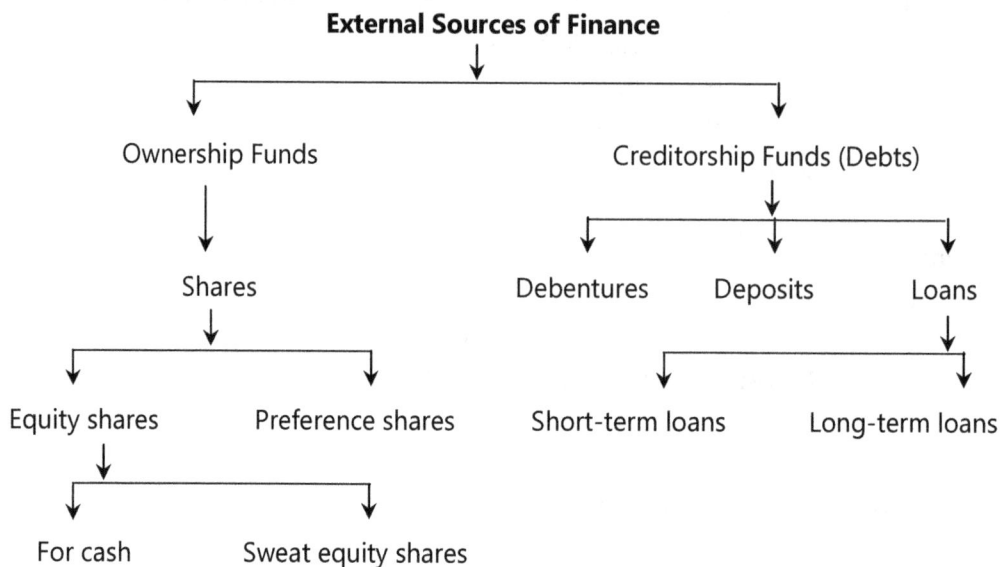

External Sources of Finance

Ownership Funds ← → Creditorship Funds (Debts)

Shares   Debentures   Deposits   Loans

Equity shares   Preference shares   Short-term loans   Long-term loans

For cash   Sweat equity shares

Fig. 2.1: External sources of finance

2.3.1 Shares

A joint stock company divides its capital into small sub-parts of equal value. These sub-parts are called shares. These shares are sold to obtain capital for the firm. Public Limited companies are allowed to issue their shares to the public, whereas Private Limited companies are prohibited from issuing their shares to the public.

Meaning and Types of Shares

Definition: Section 2(46) of the Companies Act defines, "*a share is the share in the capital of a company and includes stock except where a distinction between stock and share is expressed or implied*".

Websters' new world Dictionary states, "*A unit of ownership in a corporation, mutual fund or less commonly some other type of financial investment*".

Features of Shares

The following features of shares can be drawn from the definitions:

1. Shares confer ownership rights to the holders. That means, the shareholders have a right to get a share in the profits of the company and a claim on the assets of the company in the event of liquidation of the company, after the settlement of debts.

2. Shares have a face value and a distinct number.

3. Shares are transferable. In case of a Private Limited Company some restrictions are imposed on the transferability of shares.

4. The shares of listed companies can be bought and sold at the stock-exchange at a higher or a lower price.

5. Shares form the permanent capital of a firm, except redeemable preference shares which are repaid within a certain number of years.

   A company can also buy-back its shares from the market as per the provisions of Section 7A of the Companies (Amendment) Act, 2000. Some of the conditions are:

   - Buy-back should be out of the free reserves of the company or securities premium account or the proceeds of shares or other specified securities.
   - It must be authorized by the company's article and the company must pass the special resolution in the AGM of the company.
   - An amount equal to the nominal value of shares bought out of its reserves must be transferred to an account called Capital Redemption Reserve.

6. Companies may pay dividend as a return for investment, to the shareholders. A company is under no legal obligation to pay the dividend. On preference shares, the rate of dividend is fixed and on the ordinary shares, the rate of dividend is determined by the Directors of the company. Shareholders can reduced the rate of Dividend as declared by the Directors of the company, but cannot increase the rate.

7. The shareholders enjoy limited liability. That means they can be called upon to pay only the unpaid balance on the shares held by them and no more. Their private properties are not liable for the liabilities of the company. This can be explained with the help of the following example: Suppose 'A' holds 1,000 shares of XYZ Ltd. The issue price of the said share is say ₹ 10. If he has already paid ₹ 8 each on the shares held by him, his liability will be limited to ₹ 2,000 only i.e. 1,000 shares × 4.2.

(A) (i) Ordinary Shares / Equity Shares

No company can come into existence without equity capital. The equity shareholders are the legal owners of the company. Equity share capital represents permanent capital of a company since a company need not repay the money so raised. These shares posses the following features besides possessing the general features of shares:

1. **Voting Rights:** Equity shares carry with them the right to vote on important occasions. These voting rights help the shareholder to exercise control over the management of the company. Each share carries one vote. Thus, equity shareholders enjoy proportionate voting rights. The occasions on which voting rights are exercised are:
   - For changing authorised capital;
   - For altering the memorandum of the association;
   - On the occasion of election of Directors;
   - For changing the objectives of the company.

The voting rights may be exercised in person or by proxy. A proxy is a ballot that allows shareholders to caste their vote at an annual general meeting or without attending the meeting. A proxy gives a designated person the right to vote on behalf of a shareholder at a company meeting.

2. **Claim on Profits of the Company:** The ordinary shareholders are entitled to the residual profits of the company i.e. the income left after deducting all expenses, taxes and preference dividend. The directors may distribute the residual profits among the shareholders in the form of cash dividends or may opt to retain the surplus for future expansion programmes. Retained earnings benefit the owners in the form of enhanced value of shares or increased dividend, when this is capitalised.

   The company is under no legal obligation to pay the dividend. Shareholders get dividend only when Directors declare the dividend.

3. **Claim on Assets:** As in the case with profits, the claim of the shareholder on the assets of the company is residual claim. In the event of liquidation of the company, the assets released will be used in the first instance to settle the claims of creditors such as loan, trade creditors, debenture holders etc. Then the claims of preference shareholders shall be satisfied and finally the left-over cash shall be used to pay the equity shareholders. The equity shareholders normally remain unpaid, when a company closes down due to business failure.

4. **Preemptive Rights:** The existing shareholder of a company have preemptive right to hold same proportion of shares, in the event of fresh shares. This is called 'Right' or 'Right Share'. In other words, the company must offer the new shares to the existing shareholders. This right of shareholders, prevents dilution of their stake and control in the company.

   Preventive rights are given by way of 'subscription warrant', that spells out the number of new shares the shareholder is entitled to buy. The shareholder may buy the share, or allow the right to lapse or sell the right at the stock market.

5. **Right to control:** 'Control' means the power to influence the management of the company. Although shareholders do not take part in the day to day management of the company, they can indirectly influence the policies of the company. They have the right to elect the Directors, through the exercise of voting rights. They can even remove the Directors if their performance is not up to their expectation. Ordinary shareholders are able to control the management of the company through their voting rights and to maintain proportionate ownership.

Merits and Demerits of Equity Financing

Equity capital is the most important long-term source of financing. It offers the following advantages:

Advantages to the company

1. **Permanent Capital:** Ordinary shares are irredeemable. The holders of these shares are not repaid their investment during the course of business. It is a source of permanent capital. It is repaid only in the event of liquidation of the company, after settlement of the dues of debenture holders, all current liabilities and dues of preference shareholders. If the funds are available, the shareholders are paid or else they remain unpaid.

2. **No dividend burden:** Company is under no legal obligation to pay dividend on these shares. The directors may declare the dividend considering the liquidity position, availability of net profits, opportunities of investment available to the company etc.

3. **No charge on assets:** In order to raise funds through equity shares, the company need not create any charge against its assets. Hence, assets remain free of charge.

4. **Easy borrowing:** Equity capital provides finance base to the company. Lending institutions consider the equity base of a borrowing company before lending. Since issue of equity share doesn't create charge on the assets, a company can borrow against the security of these assets.

5. **Large amounts:** Face value of ordinary shares is very small and hence, people with small savings can also buy these shares. This makes raising of large amounts of finance possible.

Advantages to the Shareholders

1. **Voting rights:** Shareholders of ordinary shares enjoy voting rights. This gives them the power to control the management of the company.

2. **Pre-emptive rights:** Pre-emptive rights allow the shareholders to maintain the proportionate ownership. Company must offer the new shares to the existing shareholders.

3. **Transfer of Shares:** Shareholders can transfer the shares and leave the company whenever they want. The shares of a Public Ltd. Company are easily transferable, hence the shareholders can sell the shares when the market price is high and can enjoy capital gains (make profit).

4. **High dividend and earning:** When the company is doing well, these shareholders earn high dividends and enjoy high EPS (Earnings Per Share).

5. **Face value is small:** Since the face value is small and issue price is not very high, shareholders may find it easy to buy these shares.

Disadvantages or Limitations of Equity Financing

Equity financing suffers from the following limitations:

Disadvantages to the Company

1. **Heavy cost:** The floating cost is very high. Besides, there is inconvenience associated with equity financing. The dividend is not deductible out of profit for tax purposes unlike interest on borrowings.

2. **No Trading on Equity:** A company depending on equity finance cannot pass on the advantages of trading on equity to its shareholders. This may lead to over-capitalisation.

3. **Concerning of shares:** The control of the company can be manipulated through concerning of shares by a group of shareholders for their personal advantage at the cost the company's interest.

4. **Fear of Transfer of control:** Conservative management may avoid issue of additional shares in the fear of possibility of transfer of control from existing shareholder to the new holders of equity.

Disadvantages to the Shareholders

Equity shares have some disadvantages to the shareholders:

1. **Uncertain returns:** Company need not pay dividend to its shareholders, so small investors and retired people who have bought equity shares may be uncertain about the earnings.

2. **Principle amount:** The equity shares are not redeemable during the life of a company. Even on liquidation they may not be repaid, if funds are insufficient.

3. **Fall in EPS:** Preemptive rights give the existing shareholder to buy more shares. But further issue of shares may bring down the EPS, if the additional funds do not generate additional profits immediately.

4. **Dilution of ownership:** The issue of new shares may dilute the ownership and control. The preemptive rights may not be exercised by the existing shareholders for want of liquidity.

Sweat Equity Shares

Sweat equity shares refer to those equity shares which are issued by a company to its employees or directors at a discount for considerations other than cash. They may be issued for providing know-how or making available rights in the nature of intellectual property rights or value addition, by whatever name it is called.

Such shares can be issued if following conditions are satisfied:

1. It can be issued for a class of shares already issued by the company.
2. The issue must be authorized by a special resolution passed by the company in its general meeting.
3. Not less than one year must have elapsed since the date on which the company was entitled to commence business, and
4. In case the company's equity shares are listed on a recognised stock-exchange, then the seat issue must be made in accordance with the regulations of Securities and Exchange Board of India (SEBI).

(A) (ii) Preference Shares

Preference shares, like ordinary shares, confer ownership rights to its holders who are entitled to fixed rates of dividend out of the profits of the company. These are called preference shares as the holders of these shares enjoy the following preferences over other classes of shareholders.

*   They enjoy preference as regards dividends i.e. before any dividend is paid to the holders of ordinary shares.
*   The rate of dividend is fixed and hence the rate of preference dividend is not based on the discretion of the Directors of the company.
*   In the event of liquidation of the company, preference shareholders enjoy preference as regards to repayment of their capital.

Types of Preference Shares

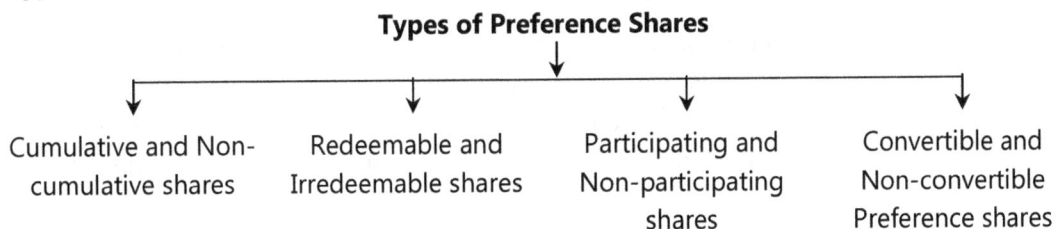

Types of Preference Shares

Cumulative and Non-cumulative shares	Redeemable and Irredeemable shares	Participating and Non-participating shares	Convertible and Non-convertible Preference shares

Fig. 2.2: Types of Preference Shares

(a) Cumulative and Non-cumulative Preference Shares

On the basis of liability for preference dividend, there can be cumulative preference shares. The dividend on cumulative preference shares goes on accumulating, till it is declared and paid. Suppose a company doesn't declare dividend due to lack of liquid cash or profits. Then the company will have to pay dividend in the next year, for two years.

On non-cumulative preference shares such obligation doesn't exist. Hence, if company doesn't declare dividend in a year these preference shareholders cannot claim it the next year.

(b) Redeemable and Irredeemable Preference Shares

Company repays the redeemable preference shares as per the specified period and if the period is not specified then after fulfilling the required formalities. On the other hand, irredeemable preference shares are permanent source of finance to the company.

(c) Participating of Non-participating Preference Shares

Participating preference shares not only enjoy preference as regards a fixed rate of dividend but also have the right to participate / share the profits left after the equity dividend.

Non-participating preference shares get only a fixed amount of dividend.

(d) Convertible and Non-Convertible Preference Shares

The holders of Convertible Preference Shares can exercise their option to convert their shares into equity shares. On the other hand, non-convertible preference shares do not possess any such options.

Features of Preference Shares

Preference shares are often called as hybrid security. They have some features of ordinary shares and some features of debentures:

1. **Claim on income:** Preference shares has a prior claim on the profits of the company, in the sense that after the payment of interest on taxes the fixed preference dividend is payable. In case company doesn't declare dividend, the preference shareholders have to forego their dividend except cumulative preference shareholders, whose dividend accumulates till it is paid.

2. **Claim on assets:** In the event of liquidation preference shareholders have prior claim on the company's assets. The preference share claim is satisfied after that of debenture and before that of ordinary share. Thus, preference share is less risky both from the point of view of the shareholders and from the point of view of the company.

3. **Voting rights:** Preference shareholders generally do not have voting rights and they cannot participate in the management of the company. They may be entitled to contingent voting rights. If their dividends are outstanding for two or more years, they can nominate a member in the Board.

4. **No tax benefit:** Preference dividend is not deductible for tax purposes.

5. **No fixed maturity date:** Even in case of redeemable preference shares, the maturity date or period may not be stated. They are like 'fair weather funds'. As long as the company needs these funds, it uses and then repays the investment of preference shareholders.

6. **No risk of insolvency:** There is no risk of insolvency if the company doesn't pay dividends.

Merits of Preference Shares as a Source of Finance

Advantages for the Company

(i) **No dividend burden:** From the company's point of view there is no legal burden on the company to pay dividends. If the profits decline the company can omit to pay the dividend.

(ii) **Long-term funds:** Preference shares provide long-term funds to the company as they do not have a specified maturity date except redeemable preference shares. Thus, the fund provided by them is a perpetual loan. Company need- not provide for its redemption.

(iii) **No risk of insolvency:** Non-payment of preference dividend doesn't force the company into insolvency.

(iv) **No charge on assets:** Issue of preference shares doesn't cerate any change against assets of the company. Hence, assets are available for other sources of finance such as term loans.

(v) **No dilution of ownership and control:** Although preference shareholders are one of the owners of the company, they do not enjoy any voting rights hence there is no dilution of ownership and control of ordinary shareholders.

(vi) **Stronger financial base:** Preference shares capital provides sound financial base to the company. This increases the ability of the company to borrows as the preference share capital reduces the risk of the lenders.

Advantages to the Preference Shareholders

1. **Fixed Dividend:** The rate of preference dividend is fixed and is not decided by the directors of the company.

2. **Preferences:** The holders of preference shareholders enjoy preference with regard to their dividend and with respect to repayment of their investment.

3. **Right to nominate:** In case of non-payment of preference dividend the preference shareholders can nominate their member in the Board of Directors.

Disadvantages to the Company

1. **Non-deductibility of liquid:** Preference dividend is not tax deductible. That is, it involves cash outflow in the form of dividend as well as in the form of additional tax when compared to debenture interest or interest on term loans.

2. **Commitment to pay dividend:** Though company need not pay preference dividend, but practically speaking the dividend must be paid to protect the image of the company and also because equity dividend cannot be paid unless preference dividend is paid.

3. **Dilution of the claim of ordinary shareholders:** Preference shareholders dilute the claim of the equity shareholders over the assets of the company.

Disadvantages to the Preference Shareholders

1. **No voting rights:** Although they are owners of the company and are paid out of the profits of the company, they have no say in the management and control of the company as they do not have voting rights.

2. **Rates of dividend fixed:** Even in those years when company earns huge amount of profit, the preference shareholders are entitled to only fixed rate of dividend.

3. **Redemption:** Whenever company is not in need of funds, they are paid back their investment, against their wish sometimes.

At the time of re-organisation the company can convert its preference shares into equity and vice-versa.

2.3.2 Debentures

A debenture is a creditorship security issued by a company. Interest at a fixed rate is payable on debentures. According to the Companies Act, the term debenture includes *"debenture stock, bonds and any other security of a company whether constituting a charge of the assets of the company or not"*. An alternative form of debenture in India is bond. Bonds are mostly issued by Public Sector Companies in India.

Features of Debentures

1. **Interest rate:** The interest rate on a debenture is fixed. This interest rate is called the 'coupon rate of interest'. It indicates the rate of interest payable on the face value of debenture periodically, annually, semi-annually or quarterly. Payment of interest is legally binding on the company. The interest is tax deductible for the company. But the Debenture holders may have to pay tax on the interest income as per the Income-Tax Rules of the Government. Public Sector undertaking may issue tax-free bonds i.e. the interest income herewith is not taxable.

2. **Maturity:** Debentures are issued with a specific maturity periods (except irredeemable debentures). The redemption value may be at par, discount, or premium as stated at the time of issue. The redemption may be redeemed in installment or at one time. Companies create provisions for their redemption, e.g. sinking fund.

3. **Redemption:** Redemption of debentures can be by the creation of sinking funds or by buying the debentures at market price to cancel those. The buy-back price may be more than the par value of the debenture.

4. **Indenture or trust deed:** A legal agreement is entered into between the company issuing debenture and the debenture trustee who represents the debenture holders. This agreement is called the 'indenture'. The debenture trustee is responsible for protecting the interest of the debenture holders. A financial institution or a bank or an insurance company or a firm of the attorneys is appointed as a trustee. The trust deed contains the rights of debenture holders, rights of the issuing company and the responsibilities of trustees.

5. **Security:** Generally the debentures are issued by creating charge against the assets of the company. The charge may be fixed charge or a floating charge. When the asset is specified it is fixed charge. In the event of failure of the company to pay the debenture, the debenture trustee can seize the said property, on behalf of the debenture holders. Company cannot dual feely in those specified assets without the consent of the lender.

   A floating charge may be created to secure the interest of the debenture holders. This charge is not attached to any specific assets but floats over all the company's assets, until crystallization, i.e. until some event (typically winding-up) causes it to become fixed. This type of charges are suitable for 'current assets' whose values keep fluctuating. In the event of company liquidation fixed-charge holders are paid even before the preferential creditors (like government dues) and floating charge holders are paid after the payment to preferential creditors.

6. **Claim over assets of the company:** In the event of liquidation of the company, debenture holders are paid before payments are made to preference and equity shareholders. Debenture holders secured by assets of the company are paid prior to the debenture holders not having any security.

Types of Debentures

The various types of debentures are:

(i) **Convertible and Non-Convertible Debentures:** A Convertible Debenture can be fully or partly be converted into shares after a specified period of time. A convertible debenture may be fully convertible or partly convertible. Fully convertible debentures carry lower rates of interest than the interest rates on non-convertible debentures. The terms of agreement state the terms of the issue with regard to price and time of conversion.

   Non-convertible debentures are pure debentures. They cannot be converted into equity shares. These are repayable on maturity.

(ii) **Secured and Unsecured Debentures:** Secured debentures are secured by a charge – fixed or floating on the assets of the company. Unsecured debentures do not create any charge on the assets of the company.

(iii) **Redeemable and Perpetual Debenture:** Redeemable debentures are repaid on the maturity date, whereas perpetual debenture are source of permanent funds for the company and hence are repaid only on the winding-up of the company.

(iv) **Floating Rate Bonds:** Floating rate bonds are the ones where the coupon rate is reset periodically, based on the prevailing rates in the market.

(v) **Secured Premium notes:** In this type of bonds, the principal amount is refunded alongwith interest and 'premium' in installments. The company can pay the premium amount by changing the reserves and surplus. Such bonds allow the holders to get equity shares of the company at a price fixed before.

(vi) **Zero coupon bonds:** In zero coupon bonds, as the name suggests there is no fixed coupon rate. The maturity value is more than the issue price. The difference is treated as gain by the investors.

(vii) **Deep Discount Bonds (DDB):** There bonds are issued at a discount. These bonds are redeemed to their face value over a certain period of time. The advantage to the company is, it need not pay interest immediately. But if the interest rate falls the company may stand to lose. For example, a debenture of a face value of ₹ 1,000 may be issued at ₹ 250, for a period of 20 years. After 20 years the debenture is redeemed at its face value.

Merits and Demerits of Debenture as a Long-term Source of Finance

Merits

1. **Low cost:** It is a less costly source of finance due to the following reasons:
   - Floatation cost is less when compared to ordinary shares.
   - Interest rates are lower as these are less risky investment.
   - Interest payment is tax deductible.

2. **No dilution of ownership and control:** Debenture is a long-term source of finance. Since debenture holders do not possess voting rights it doesn't dilute the power of control by the equity shareholders. Besides these are creditorship securities, hence ownership is not diluted.

3. **Less risky:** Debentures are less risky investment for the debenture holders, as the company is under legal obligation to pay interest on it and repay the principle amount on maturity.

4. **Advantages of trading on equity:** The interest rates are low, hence a company can provide the benefits of trading on equity to its equity shareholders. Company can pay its ordinary shareholders a rate of dividend higher than the overall return on their investment.

5. **Reduction in real obligation:** During periods of inflation the repayment of the principal amount and interest payments are less in real terms, since the purchasing power of money would be less during inflation.

Demerits

1. **Fear of insolvency:** The payment of interest and repayment of the principal amount is legal binding on the company. In case company fails to meet these obligations, the debenture holder can file a suit for winding-up of the company.

2. **Cash outflows:** Payment of debenture interest and repayment of principal amount involves cash outflows. Company's liquidity position may get affected if proper arrangements are not made, for example, an arrangement of bank over-draft.

3. **Trust deed:** The indenture may contain the terms which may limit the company's operating flexibility.

Comparison between Shares and Debentures

Share and Debentures provide long-term finance to a company. They can be differentiated as follows:

Shares	Debentures
1. Shares are ownership securities.	Debentures are creditorship securities.
2. The return on investment on shares is dividend.	The debentures carry a right to interest at a fixed rate.
3. Shares provide permanent capital to a firm.	Debentures are a long-term source of finance and are generally repayable after a specified period of time.
4. The dividend may or may not be paid. It depends on the discretion of the Board of Directors.	A company is under a legal obligation to pay interest.
5. No change is created against the assets of the company, when shares are issued.	Debenture-holder's interest is secured by the creation of a fixed or floating charge against the assets of the company.

2.3.3 Public Deposits

Public Deposits may be accepted by companies from their Members, Directors and from the general public. The period of public deposit is a minimum of 6 months and a maximum of 3 years. Public deposits are accepted to meet the short-term requirements of the company.

Public deposits provide the following advantages:

Advantages/Merits

1. **Less Formalities:** It is easy to obtain finance through public deposits as many formalities are not involved. The company only has to advertise and inform the public about its interest in public deposits.

2. **Less costly:** It is a less costly method for raising short-term as well as medium term funds required by the business.

3. **No charge created:** Public deposits are unsecured and hence, no charge is created against the assets of the company. Assets remain free of charge.

4. **Trading on equity:** Since the interest on the deposits and the period of repayment of the deposit is fixed, company can take the advantage of trading on equity. Company can pay a higher rate of return to the equity shareholders over and above its rate of return on investment.

Limitations/Disadvantages

1. **Good reputation:** Although formalities involved in issue of public deposits are less complicated, it is difficult to raise funds through public deposits. Since charge is not created against any assets of the company, investor may be skeptical about the capacity of the company to pay interest and repay the principal amount. Only reputed companies can use this source of finance.

2. **Premature withdrawal:** Public deposits can be withdrawn by the depositors before the maturity date. Funds generated through this method are uncertain because even a slight doubt about the companies ability can result in premature withdrawal. Company can find it difficult to respond to the demand of the deposit holder. This makes this source of finance uncertain.

2.3.4 Borrowing from Banks

Commercial Banks are a major source of finance to industries and commerce. Banks normally provide short-term credit for financing working capital needs. Term loans are mainly extended by development and financing institutions also called as 'Development Banks'.

Short-term Financing

Short-term loans are obtained for working capital requirements. Commercial Banks in India provide only short-term and medium-term loans.

Types of Advances

1. **Loans:** 'Loans' refers to the money lent on condition that it is repaid, either in installments or all at once, on agreed dates and usually the borrower pays the lender an agreed rate of interest. The loan may be advanced with or without security.

   The bank either makes the lump-sum payment to the borrower or credit his deposit account with the loan advanced. It is given for a fixed period of time and at an agreed rate of interest. Rate of interest may be fixed. The interest has to be paid on the whole amount of loan sanctioned irrespective of whether loan amount has been used or not.

   The rate of interest on loan is lower than other forms of advances made by the banker because it involves lower cost of maintenance.

   Bank loan may be 'term loan' or 'demand loan'. Term loan has to be repaid after the stated period of time or in installments alongwith interest. Demand loan on the other hand is repayable on demand.

2. **Cash Credits:** A cash credit is an arrangement by which a bank credits the borrowers account with the amount of advance sanctioned. Interest is charged on the amount used by the borrower and not on the whole amount sanctioned.

Usually cash credit is allowed against security of commodities hypothecated or pledged with the bank.

(a) **Hypothecation:** In case of hypothecation the goods used as security for borrowing, remain in possession of the borrower. Bank has access to the goods hypothecated. The borrower has to provide the Bank with information regarding the stock movements.

(b) **Pledge:** In case of pledge, the goods are placed in custody of the bank. The borrower losses his right to deal with them.

3. **Overdrafts:** A customer holding a current account may be allowed to overdraw his current account with or without security. The customer is required to pay interest on the amount actually overdrawn.

4. **Discounting of Bills:** The banks also provide discounting facility. Companies can sell their bills of exchange to the banks who purchase it at a discounted price. On the maturity date bank makes arrangements to collect the bill amount from the acceptors of bills. It is a kind of advance to the customers as they get money on the bill before the due date. The discount includes interest as well as bankers gain. The banks may discount the bill with or without security from the debtor.

Advantages and Disadvantages of Short-term Credit from Commercial Banks

Advantages

1. **Cheaper:** Short-term credit from commercial banks is generally cheaper as compared to any other short-term finance.

2. **Accessibility:** There are large number of commercial banks with their branches spread over. Commercial banks readily lend credit.

3. **Special schemes:** As per the instructions of the RBI, commercial banks provide credit at concessional rate under special schemes.

4. **Advice:** Commercial banks guide the businesses in respect of new ventures, appropriates sources of finance etc.

Disadvantages

1. **Formalities:** Financing through bank credit involves lot of formalities and signing of a number of documents, which is time-consuming and involves cost.

2. **Security demanded:** Bank demands security for loan, hence, firms may not like to depend on commercial banks for their short-term financial requirements.

2.3.5 Term Loans

Term loans are an important source of long-term finance for a firm. These are loans borrowed directly from the banks and financial institutions, for medium and long-term periods, i.e. for a period of 1 to 5 years and beyond 5 years to 15 to 20 years. Term loans are generally obtained for financing large expansion, modernisation or diversification of projects.

Features of Term Loans

The basic features of term loans are discussed below:

1. **Maturity:** Banks and specialised financial institutions provide term loans. Commercial banks advance loans for a period of 3 to 5 years and Financial Institutions (FIs) provide term loans for a longer period generally for a period of 6 to 10 years. Sometimes moratorium of 1 to 2 years is provided. Moratorium is an agreement between a creditor and a debtor to allow additional firms for settlement of a debt. This period is allowed to the firms with the intention to give them time to make the necessary financial arrangements to settle their liabilities.

2. **Private Placement:** Debentures and bonds are placed for public subscription. On the other hand, term loans are privately placed. The advantage of private placement is that the firm and the Bank of FIs can negotiate the term of loan, to the advantage of both the parties. Besides there is no floatation cost and no under-writing commission payable.

3. **Security:** Term loans are secured by the lending institutions by creating a charge against the assets of the company. Lender may create a fixed charge or a floating charge. Fixed charge is created on specific assets of the company. Fixed charge is created by paying heavy stamp duty. Floating charge on the other hand, is a general mortgage covering all assets of the company. Company cannot deal with the assets with fixed charges freely, lenders, approval is required.

   Security, i.e. the assets to which a lender can have as resources in the event of default by the borrower, can be primary security or collateral (secondary) security. Primary security is the security of those assets which are bought specifically out of the concerned term loan. But when terms loans are secured by the present and future assets of the company, it is called collateral security.

4. **Covenant:** Covenants are the rules on loan agreement that require certain financial conditions to be met or prohibit other financial actions by the borrower. A covenant may limit how much additional debt can be issued, require financial targets such as sales and earnings to be met, limit the payment of dividends and require certain each levels be maintained. If a covenant is violated, then the bank or loan issuer can require that the loan is repaid immediately.

5. **Convertibility:** Financial institutions provide huge sums of money as loan. In order to have an access to management of the company, the loan agreement may require that a part or whole of loan be converted into equity share.

6. **Refinance Facility:** Commercial Banks are granted refinance facility from Industrial Development Bank of India on the term loans granted by them.

7. **Project Oriented Approach:** Financial institutions provide term lending after taking up detailed appraisal of each project. The loan is sanctioned only when the project satisfies their tests.

Merits of Term Loans

1. These loans are privately placed and hence it is possible to negotiate terms of finance, to suit the project in question.

2. Like debenture interest, interest on term loans is also tax deductible.

3. They are an important source of long-term finance for a firm.

Demerits of Term Loans

1. Company has to provide security of its assets. It cannot deal with assets with fixed charges as it wishes.

2. Financial institutions, in order to protect their interest, put a number of restrictions on the functions of the borrowing firm. The firm is required to provide information periodically to the financial institutions.

2.3.6 Bridge Financing

It is a short-term financing is used as a stop-gap measure until medium or long-term funding can be arranged. It is also called as 'bridge loan'. There might be a gap between sanctioning of a term loan and its disbursement to the borrower, by a Financial Institution. In order to prevent the delay in starting the project, a bridge loan may be taken from a commercial bank against mortgage of the assets of the company. These loans are repaid as soon as loan disbursements are received from the Financial Institutions.

2.3.7 Loan Syndication

Sometimes a project of a company may be financed by two or more banks or financial institutions. This is called loan syndication. In such a case one of the institutions may become a lead institution and bring about co-ordination in the financing arrangement of different financial institution or banks.

2.4 Internal Sources of Finance

Introduction

Internal sources of finance are generated from within a firm out of its business operations. The profits earned by a firm belong to its owners and hence must be paid to the owners of a business. In case of a company form of business, there is no legal obligation to distribute the profit earned to the owners in the form of cash dividend. Companies aiming at growth and expansion do not pay cash dividends as they would like to use the profits for reinvestment. This is also known as 'ploughing back of profits'. Internal sources of finance are less costly as there is no floatation cost involved. Further, there is no obligation of servicing it i.e. no interest payment involved and is a convenient method of financing. In connection with internal source of financing the concepts given below must be understood.

2.4.1 Reserves and Surplus

"It is a part of capital of company, other than share capital, arising out of retained profit or from the issue of shares at more than its nominal value i.e. share premium". Some of the reserves represent the profits not distributed and some of it is not distributable as per law.

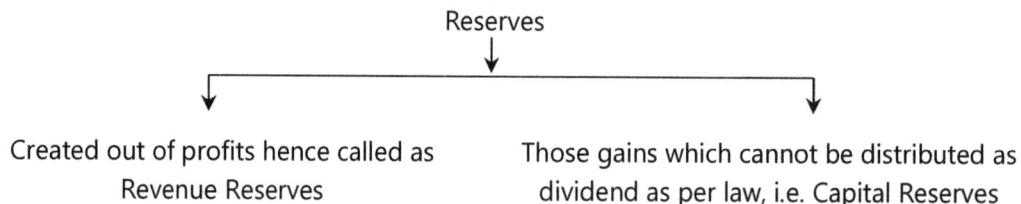

Reserves

Created out of profits hence called as Revenue Reserves	Those gains which cannot be distributed as dividend as per law, i.e. Capital Reserves

1. Revenue Reserves

Revenue reserves are the reserves created after profits, i.e. by transfer of profits to certain reserves, without distributing the same as dividend. Every company in India is required by Companies Act, 1955 to transfer a certain percentage of profit, upto to 10% of current year profit to Reserves. These reserves are distributable in the sense company can use it for distribution of dividend. Thus, revenue reserves consist of a company's accumulated realised profits after deducting all realised losses, except for any part of the net realised profit that has been previously distributed or capitalised.

Examples are:

- General reserve
- Dividend
- Reserve Fund
- Profit and Loss Account
- Insurance Fund etc.

2. Capital Reserves

Capital Reserves on the other hand represent those reserves which may be created out of profits but expressly stated in the Companies Act, as undistributable and other profits which are not generated out of regular business operations like share premium, which represents gain on issue of shares when issue price is more than the nominal value of share (Share premium = Issue Price − Face value of Shares). These reserves cannot be used for dividend purposes rather can be used for redemption of shares and debentures, for declaration of Bonus shares, for writing off capital losses etc.

Examples:

- Share Premium A/c
- Capital Reserve
- Development Rebate Reserve
- Profit prior to incorporation
- Share Forfeiture A/c

3. Reserves Vs Provisions

A distinction must be drawn between reserves and provisions in order to understand the meaning of reserves:

Table 2.1: Distinction between Reserves and Provisions

Reserves	Provisions
• Reserves are surpluses not yet distributed or not distributable.	• Provisions represent the amount set aside out of profits for a known liability or for the diminution in the value of an asset.
• Reserves arise by way of appropriation of profit or by way of certain transactions like issues of shares at premium, balance in the share forfeiture account after the re-issue of forfeited shares etc.	• Provisions form a part of profit and loss account implying they are charges against profits. Provisions for known liability, irrespective of whether company earns profits or not.
• Reserves are created with the object of creating funds for growth and expansion, or to stabilise dividend or to declare dividend in future, whenever the profits earned are insufficient to declare dividend.	• Provisions are created for a known liability, for which the amount is unknown. When the actual liability materialises it is adjusted against the provision and balance if any is added to the credit side of Profit and Loss A/c (Profit and Loss Appropriation A/c in case of provision for taxation)
• Reserves are treated as part of capital of the company.	• Provisions are treated as liabilities.
• **Examples:** Share Premium A/c General Reserve A/c Dividend Equalisation A/c Reserve etc.	• **Examples:** Bad debt provision Depreciation provision Income-tax provision etc.

2.4.2 Bonus Shares

Bonus shares refer to the shares issued by a company to its existing shareholders on the pro-rata basis, in addition to dividend. These shares are issued out of the 'Reserves' of the company. Shareholders are not to pay for it. It is also termed as capitalisation of profits. The number of shares received by a shareholder depend on the level of shareholding prior to the bonus issues. The number of 'Bonus Shares' is usually one share for a specified number of shares held before the issue. For example, if the specified number is four, this would be denoted as a 1 : 4 Bonus issue i.e., one bonus share against 4 shares held. It is also possible to have 2 : 1 bonus, when two shares are issued for every one share held. The total number of shares outstanding increases and the reserves decrease.

1. **Impact of Bonus Size**
    1. Bonus shares increase the total number of outstanding shares.
    2. It doesn't change the total capital of the firm. It only changes its form. The capital which was in the form of reserves and surplus is converted into capital.
    3. There is no change in total value of shares held by the shareholders. The reserves and surpluses belong to the shareholders only. The same profits were converted into shares and distributed to them. It doesn't change their proportion of ownership.
    4. There is no change in the capital structure of the company. Since there is no change in the debt-equity ratio.
    5. The increase in the number of shares without a change in the net income of the company will lead to a fall in the EPS. But the total earnings of the shareholders do not change.

The impact of Bonus issue can be analysed with the help of the following example:

Illustration:

Following is the capital structure of 'ABC' Co.

	₹
Paid-up Share Capital (2,00,000 shares of ₹ 10)	20,00,000
Share Premium	5,00,000
Reserves and Surplus	10,00,000
Total networth	35,00,000

Company pays bonus in the ratio of 1: 10, meaning one bonus share is issued against 10 shares held. That again means company is making a Bonus issue of 20,000 shares of ₹ 10 each.

After the issue the capital would look like this:

	₹
Paid-up Share Capital (2,20,000 shares of ₹ 10)	22,00,000
Share Premium	5,00,000
Reserves and Surplus (10,00,000 – 2,00,000)	8,00,000
Total networth	35,00,000

It is assumed that the net earnings of the company are ₹ 4,00,000.

1. It may be noted that the networth of the company has not changed post Bonus issue.
2. Total number of shares has increased from 2,00,000 shares of 2,20,000 shares.
3. EPS falls immediately after bonus issues if there is no change in the earnings of the company.

$$\text{EPS (Prior to Bonus issue)} = \frac{4,00,000}{2,00,000} = ₹\ 2$$

$$\text{EPS (after Bonus issue)} = \frac{4,00,000}{2,20,000} = 1.82$$

2. Advantages of Bonus Issue

It may be observed from the illustration that no major change takes place due to Bonus issue. Some advantages are associated with the issue which makes companies declare Bonus.

1. Bonus issue increases the number of shares traded in the stock exchange which promotes active trading in the shares of the company.

2. Bonus issues brings the market price within the normal range, i.e. at reasonable level.

3. The most important advantage of the Bonus issue is that it has a favourable psychological impact on the shareholders and investors. It gives an indication of company's growth.

4. It helps the company conserve its cash as Bonus is issued out of undistributed profits. It may increase the share price and thereby the wealth of the shareholders.

5. Bonus issue improves the prospect of raising additional funds through issues of Debentures.

6. The shareholders will get extra dividend in future even if company declares same amount of each dividend per share.

3. Provisions of Companies Act concerning Bonus Issue

According to the Companies Act, 1966, a bonus issue can be made by a company if the following conditions are satisfied:

1. The Articles of Association of the company must permit issue of Bonus Shares.

2. The Bonus must be approved by the members in the General meeting.

3. The company has sufficient undistributed profits.

4. The issue is as per the guidelines issued by the Securities Exchange of India (SEBI).

4. Guidelines of Bonus Issue

SEBI has issued new bonus guidelines on 13.04.1994. The Board of Directors of the company intending to issue Bonus shares must follow the guidelines stated below:

1. The existing listed companies are required to forward a certificate duly signed by the issuer and counter-signed by its statutory auditor or by a company secretary (practicing) that the terms and conditions stated in the guidelines have been compiled with.

2. A company, which has to convert the fully or partly convertible debentures or per terms, cannot issue Bonus shares without extending the same benefits to convertible debenture holders.

3. The bonus issue is made out of free reserves built out of genuine profits or share premium collected in cash only.

4. Revaluation reserves created out of revaluation of fixed assets cannot be utilised for Bonus issue.

5. The bonus issue cannot be made in lieu of dividend.

6. The bonus issue cannot be made unless the partly paid-up shares, if any, are fully paid-up.

7. Company has not defaulted in payment of interest or principal in respect of its debts.

8. Company has not failed to pay its statutory dues.

9. Within six months of the approval the Board of Directors, Bonus issue must be made.

10. The Articles of Association of the Company must provide for the capitalisation of reserve etc. or else the company must alter the articles by passing a special resolution at its general body meeting.

11. If after the bonus tissue, the subscribed and paid-up capital exceed the authorised share capital, a resolution shall be passed by the company at its general body meeting for increasing the authorised capital.

2.4.3 Retained Earnings

Corporate earnings that are not paid out as dividend are called retained earnings. They are also called as undistributed profits or surplus. The net profit available for distribution is less than any distribution made as dividend is retained earnings. It is not a method of financing, but is a source of finance. The retained earnings or undistributed profits refer to the accumulated profits of the company which can be used to finance its development activities. This process of using profits is called ploughing back of profits.

2.4.4 Dividend Policy

Dividend is that part of profits of a company which is distributed amongst its shareholders. According to the Institute of Chartered Accountants of India *"dividend is a distribution to shareholders out of profits or reserves available for this purpose"*. Dividend is normally expressed as an amount per share on the par value of the share. If 15% dividend is declared on ₹ 10 par value share, the dividend would amount to ₹ 1.50 per share. Dividend involves outflow of cash.

Dividend Yield: Dividend yield is the percentage of Dividend on the market value of shares. Shareholders are more interested in the Dividend yield.

$$\text{Dividend yield} = \frac{\text{Dividend per share}}{\text{Market price per share}} \times 100$$

The Directors of a company declare dividend.

(I) Types of Forms of Dividend

(i) **Preference and Equity Dividend:** Preference dividend is payable on the preference share of a company. Its percentage is fixed. Equity dividend on the other hand, is decided by the Board of Directors on the ordinary shares of the company. It may change from year to year depending upon the profits earned, availability of cash, dividend policy of the company etc. Equity shareholders approve the rate of dividend in the general meeting. They can reduce it but cannot ask for a higher rate of dividend.

(ii) **Final Dividend and Interim Dividend:** Final dividend is declared at the company's AGM together with the annual financial results. A smaller interim dividend accompanies the interim statement of the company affairs, six months before the AGM.

(iii) **Cash Dividend and Stock Dividend:** Most companies pay dividend in cash. A company must have enough cash in its bank account when cash dividends are declared. If cash or bank balance falls short of requirement, company may borrow the needed money. A cash dividend reduces both the cash as well as reserves of the company. That means on the asset's side, current asset is reduced leading to a fall in the working capital of the firm and on the liability side it reduces the total capital, i.e. net worth of the company. It thus brings about a change in the long-term as well as short-term solvency of a firm. One of the ways to measure long-term solvency is Debt: Equity ratio. With a reduction in equity, the debt proportion in the capital structure increases. Further a decrease in cash reduces the current asset of the company and this leads to decrease in the current ratio of the company and if money is borrowed to pay dividend the current liability will increase, causing the current ratio to fall further.

Companies may declare stock dividend of capitalising its profits. This is called Bonus shares. Bonus shares are issued in addition to cash dividend. Issue of Bonus shares increases the total number of outstanding shares. It doesn't involve cash outflow. Hence, it doesn't cause any change in the short-term liquidity of the company. Further, issue of Bonus shares changes the form of capital i.e. from 'Reserve' to 'Share Capital'. It doesn't change the capital structure of the company. Hence, Bonus issue doesn't alter the long-term solvency of a company.

1. Dividend Policy Approaches

Dividend decision is one of the important decisions of financial management. Dividend policy refers to the course of action or principle followed by a firm while determining the proportion of profits to be distributed as dividend and the proportion to be maintained as Reserve for future use.

Dividend can be a source of long-term finance as well as of share holders wealth maximisation. When looked at as a source of finance, dividend will be paid only when a firm doesn't have investment opportunities. A growing firm will need finance for its expansion programmes. Issues of shares etc. can bring the needed funds but these sources are expensive as they involve floatation cost. Besides they may interfere with control and management of the firm. Internal source of financing is less costly. A company adopting this approach would declare and distribute cash dividend only when investment opportunities decrease. The profits left after transferring the needed amount to reserve will be distributed as profit. In this sense dividend is the residual profit.

On the other hand firms aiming at wealth maximisation, would pay dividend because in present uncertain and imperfect capital market shareholders prefer present dividend to future dividend and capital again. This means payment of dividend will have a psychological impact on the investors. A company declaring dividend would be preferred by the investors. Hence the prices of shares would increase and the wealth of the shareholders will also increase. As per this approach a company would decide about dividend first and the residual profits would be transferred to Reserves.

When a firm increases the retained profits, it pays less dividend. Due to the imperfection and uncertainty in the capital market, shareholders and investors, do not approve of low dividend and this may adversely affect the market value per share. On the other hand, when dividends are increased, the market will respond favourable, but firm forgoes its investment opportunities for want of funds.

The management of a firm must strike a proper balance between the two approaches and evolve an optimum dividend policy.

2. **Reasons for Declaring Dividend**

   The reasons for paying dividends can be stated as follows:

   (i) **Investor Preference for Dividends:** Investors of a company might prefer dividend. Small investors, retired old persons holding shares in the company and investors preferring present income to future income, are more interested in receiving cash dividends. Company pays dividend in the form of return on their investment.

   (ii) **Information:** Information about declaration of dividend sends positive signals in the capital market. Dividend payment presupposes a sound liquidity position and at the same time implies that company is profit-making. Media carries the information, which serves as a mode of earning reputation for the company.

   (iii) **Dividend as a return on Investment:** Dividend is a return on the investment made by the firm. The shareholders invest in the company with expectation of returns. Hence, payment of dividend fulfills their desire to have income.

   (iv) **Excess Cash:** When a firms' cash reserves are high when compared to the standards, it may distribute cash dividend. Excess availability of cash may cause misuse of funds of the company.

3. Dividend Decision

Dividend decision is a complex issue. A firm may have to consider a number of factors while determining its dividend policy. A list of such factors have been discussed below:

(i) **Expectations of the Shareholders:** Shareholders of a company may consist of those who want periodical, certain returns on their investment and those who want to earn capital gain through appreciation in the market price of the shares held by them. Investors group may consist of small shareholders, retained persons, wealthy investors, institutional investors etc. Most of the small shareholders, retired persons and institutional investors prefer regular cash dividends. They want the company to follow a stable dividend policy. On the other hand, wealthy investors want to minimise their tax burden hence prefer capital gain. Same is the case with large investors who hold large number of shares in the company. Thus, different groups have conflicting interest.

Besides it may not be easy to know the preferences of the shareholders in a widely held company.

The Board of Directors should adopt such a dividend policy which gives some consideration to the interest of each of the groups comprising substantial proportion of shareholders. Besides, dividend policy once adopted should be continued as long as it does not interfere with the financial needs of the company.

(ii) **Financial needs of the Company:** Financial needs refers to the investment needs of the company. If the company has profitable investment opportunities, it may need finance. Retained earnings are convenient and low cost sources of finance. Hence, company would pay less cash dividend and rather retain the major part of its net profits. Company has not only considered its investment opportunities but also, the expected return on its investment. If overall return of the company is less than the expected rate of return of the shareholders, then it would be better to distribute cash dividend. The required rate of return is the return on the investment opportunity of the shareholder elsewhere. In other words, it represents the opportunity cost of the shareholders. Only when company's overall return on investment is higher than the return on personal investment, that company should retain its earnings.

(iii) **Legal restrictions:** The Directors are not legally compelled to declare dividends. No dividend can be declared without providing for depreciation out of the profits of the company. Dividends can be paid out of the current profits or the past accumulated profits or money provided by the Central or State Governments for the purpose of payment of Dividend. Dividend cannot be paid out of capital.

(iv) **Contractual Restrictions:** When companies borrow Term loans, the lenders may impose some restrictions on dividend payments to protect their interest. Company will have to abide by the restrictions imposed by the loan agreement.

(v) **Liquidity position:** The payment of dividend results in cash outflow. A company may have sufficient earnings to declare dividend, it may not have sufficient cash to pay dividend. Such problems are faced by growing companies. Matured companies may not face problems of liquidity .

(vi) **Desire to Control:** If the existing shareholders want to retain their ownership and control over the company, they may not like the company to raise finance through issue of shares. That implies, company should pay less dividend and depend on internal sources of finance.

On the other hand, if the Directors and shareholders do not have a strong desire to control, then company may declare cash dividends.

(vii) **Nature of Earnings:** A company earning cannot pay high rate of dividend out of wind-fall profits. A company enjoying stable income can afford to pay high rate of dividend. On the other hand, companies facing fluctuations in earning would declare low dividend.

(viii) **Access to Capital Markets:** Accessibility to capital markets is an important consideration in dividend decision-making. A growing company, with a tight liquidity position can declare high rates of dividend if it has easy accessibility to capital markets.

(ix) **Inflation:** During periods of inflation, cash outflow takes place when price levels are low or when the value of money is high and cash inflows takes place when prices rise. Thus, the amount of investment in a project might not be recovered in the real sense. In order to replace the assets to make further investments, company might not declare cash dividend and rather utilise the profits and cash reserves to keep the capital intact.

(x) **Desire to stabilise Dividend:** If company desires to have stable rate of dividend, the company may declare dividend as per the past decisions.

4. Stability of Dividend

Stability of dividend is considered a desirable policy by the management of most companies. Stable dividend may have a positive impact on the market price of the share. 'Stability of dividend' may mean any of the following:

(i) Constant dividend per share or dividend rate.

(ii) Constant payout.

(iii) Constant dividend per share plus extra dividend.

(i) **Constant dividend per share or dividend rate:** It means the amount of dividend on each share remains the same, irrespective of the fluctuations in the earnings, company would change the dividend per share when it reaches new levels of stable EPS. It is easy for a company, whose earning pattern shows less fluctuations, to follow this policy. Even a company whose earnings fluctuate widely can follow this policy by transferring sufficient amount of profits to Dividend Equalisation Reserve. Such company may declare dividend out of current year's profits when profits are high and from reserves when profits are low. Thus, it can pay average dividend year after year till the level of profits become high.

(ii) **Constant Payout:** Payout ratio is the ratio of dividend paid to EPS. Companies may decide to follow a constant payout ratio i.e. paying a fixed percentage of its earnings every year. According to this method, the amount of dividend will change when earnings change. In other words, amount of dividend will fluctuate in direct proportion to earnings. If company incurs losses no dividend is payable. Under this method, a part of the earning is retained. A 40% payout ratio means 40% of the earning is paid as dividend and the remaining 60% is retained. This method is simple to follow. A company with wild fluctuations in its earnings may lend up with fluctuations in the amount of dividend, which may not be approved by the small investors, retired persons etc. who want stable income.

(iii) **Small constant dividend per share plus extra dividend:** Companies with fluctuating earnings may find it difficult to pay uniform amount of dividend year after year. Such companies may fix a constant amount of dividend and pay extra dividend during a period of high profits. The fixed amount of dividend is kept at a low level, so that there is less possibility of the amount being unpaid. This keeps the expectations of the shareholders low. The extra dividend is treated as occasional earning.

2.4.4.1 Significance of Stability of Dividend

Stability of dividend has various advantages:

1. Investor knows about the Dividend policy of the company. If it matches with their preferences, they invest in the company.

2. Institutional investors are interested in having a stable income. Financial institutions are some of the largest investors in corporate securities.

3. A stable dividend policy is advantageous to the company because it helps the company to raise external finance. Stable dividend reduces speculation in the shares of the company. Shareholders' loyalty may increase and this may make it easy to raise finance by issue of further shares.

2.4.4.2 Problem of Stability of Dividend

Once stable dividend policy has been adopted by a company, any adverse change in it could seriously damage the financial reputation of the company. Thus, it would become very difficult for the company to deviate from its dividend policy.

2.5 Role of Depreciation

Depreciation is the reduction in the value of Fixed asset due to wear and tear or obsolescence over an accounting period. Depreciation reduces the book value of the asset and is changed against income of the firm in its Profit and Loss Account. Depreciation is calculated by means of a number of generally accepted techniques including the 'Straight Line Method' and the 'Diminishing Value Method'.

2.5.1 Treatment of Depreciation in Accounting

(a) Cost Accounting

Cost accounting aims at cost determination: product-wise, process-wise, department-wise etc. for cost control purposes.

Depreciation is treated as an indirect cost i.e., overhead. Depreciation of Plant and Machinery, Equipment etc. is part of Factory Overhead because these assets are used in the production process. On the other hand, Depreciation of Furniture and depreciation of show-room building etc. are treated as administration and selling overheads, respectively. Depreciation is thus a part of the total cost of a product. A company tries to recover all its cost through the sale of a product. Thus, depreciation is recovered in the form of cash or is present in the Debtors, Bills Receivable or Closing Stock (Unsold Finished Goods).

(b) Financial Accounting

Depreciation is charged against the income of the company in the Profit and Loss Account. Due to this, the profit of the company reduces, thereby reducing the tax liability. This helps in conserving the cash reserves of the company. Indirectly depreciation provides finance to the company.

In a limited sense, depreciation can be treated as a source of finance.

2.6 Merits and Demerits of Internal Sources of Finance

Financing through internal sources is termed as 'ploughing back of profits'. This method of financing has the following merits:

Merits

(i) Retained profits are convenient source of financing. Not much of formalities are required to be fulfilled to use it. No underwriting is required, no banks are to be contacted etc.

(ii)   This method of financing is least costly since it doesn't involve any floatation costs.

(iii) This method of financing is very useful for expansion and improvements.

(iv)   Use of this source of financing involves issue of bonus shares. There is no legal obligation on the part of the company to pay dividend.

Demerits

The negative consequences of internal financing can be:

(i)   Excessive use of internal financing may not provide the benefits of **'Trading on Equity'** to the shareholders of the company.

(ii)   Use of internal finance may lead to formation of **monopolies.**

(iii) Shareholders may **object** to retaining profit if they prefer cash dividend.

(iv)   Management may be able to cover up their inefficiency.

Points to Remember

- **Factors determining the choice of a source of finance:**
  (i)   Period of finance
  (ii)   Cost of funds
  (iii) Amount of finance
  (iv)   Availability of capital markets
  (v)   Shareholders expectations
  (vi)   Trading on Equity
  (vii) Risk
  (viii) Government regulations

- **Sources of Finance:** Sources of Finance can be classified as:
  (i)   On the basis of period – long term sources or short term sources
  (ii)   On the basis of ownership – owned funds or borrowed funds
  (iii) On the basis of the sources of generation of finance

- **Shares**: In financial markets, a share is a unit of account for various financial instruments including stocks (ordinary or preferential), and investments in limited partnerships, and real estate investment trusts. The common feature of all these is equity participation (limited in the case of preference shares).

- **Shares possess the following features:**
  (i)   Voting rights
  (ii)   Claim on profits of the company
  (iii) Claim on assets
  (iv)   Pre-emptive rights
  (v)   Right to control

- **Types of Preference shares:**
  (i)   Cumulative and non cumulative shares
  (ii)   Redeemable and Irredeemable shares
  (iii) Participating and non-participating shares
  (iv)   Convertible and non-convertible shares

- **Debentures:** A debenture is a document that either creates a debt or acknowledges it, and it is a debt without collateral. In corporate finance, the term is used for a medium- to long-term debt instrument used by large companies to borrow money. In some countries the term is used interchangeably with bond, loan stock or note. A debenture is thus like a certificate of loan or a loan bond evidencing the fact that the company is liable to pay a specified amount with interest and although the money raised by the debentures becomes a part of the company's capital structure, it does not become share capital.

- **Features of debentures:**
  (i)   Interest rate
  (ii) Maturity
  (iii) Redemption
  (iv) Indenture or trust deed
  (v)   Security
  (vi) Claim over assets of the company

- **Types of Debentures:**
  (i)   Convertible and non-convertible debentures
  (ii)   Secured and unsecured debentures
  (iii) Redeemable and perpetual debentures
  (iv)   Floating rate bonds
  (v)   Secured premium notes
  (vi)   Zero coupon bonds
  (vii) Deep discount bonds

- **Bridge financing:** In investment banking terms, it is a method of financing used by companies before their IPO, to obtain necessary cash for the maintenance of operations. Bridge financing is designed to cover expenses associated with the IPO and is typically short-term in nature. Once the IPO is complete, the cash raised from the offering will immediately payoff the loan liability.

- **Loan syndication:** It is the process of involving several different lenders in providing various portions of a loan. Loan syndication most often occurs in situations where a borrower requires a large sum of capital that may either be too much for a single lender to provide, or may be outside the scope of a lender's risk exposure levels. Thus, multiple lenders will work together to provide the borrower with the capital needed, at an appropriate rate agreed upon by all the lenders.

- **Types of reserves:**
  (i)   Revenue reserves
  (ii) Capital reserves

- **Bonus Share:** A bonus share is a free share of stock given to current shareholders in a company, based upon the number of shares that the shareholder already owns.

- **Retained earnings** refers to the portion of net income of a corporation that is retained by the corporation rather than distributed to shareholders as dividends, or as the amount available to the corporation for distribution to shareholders.

- Dividend policy is concerned with financial policies regarding paying cash dividend in the present or paying an increased dividend at a later stage. Whether to issue dividends and what amount, is determined mainly on the basis of the company's inappropriate profit (excess cash) and influenced by the company's long-term earning power. When cash surplus exists and is not needed by the firm, then management is expected to pay out some or all of those surplus earnings in the form of cash dividends or to repurchase the company's stock through a share buyback program.

- **Treatment of depreciation in accounting:**
    - (i)   Cost accounting
    - (ii) Financial accounting

Questions for Discussion

(I) State whether the following statements are True or False:

- (i)   Preference shareholders are entitled to receive dividend at fixed rate irrespective of the amount of profit earned by the company.
- (ii)   Private limited company is prohibited from issuing its shares to the public.
- (iii)   An equity company can pass on the benefits of trading on equity to its ordinary shareholders.
- (iv)   Participating preference shares, participate in the surplus profit of the company after adjusting equity dividend.
- (v)   Bridge finance is provided for construction purposes.
- (vi)   Cumulative preference shareholders are entitled to get the dividend for the previous year if it was not paid to them.
- (vii)   EPS stands for 'Ease in Payment Security'.
- (viii) Expectations of equity shareholders are one of the constituent part of the cost of equity capital.
- (ix)   A share is an indivisible part of the share capital of a company.
- (x)   A company can buy-back its shares and debentures.
- (xi)   There exists no difference between shares and stocks.
- (xii)   Proportionate voting rights of equity shareholders means, every shareholder has voting right.
- (xiii) Preemptive rights enable the shareholders of a company to maintain proportionate ownership.
- (xiv)   Sweat Equity Shares are issued at a discount.
- (xv)   In the event of liquidation of a company, the equity shareholders' claim on assets of the company falls net in rank, to the claim of preference shareholders.
- (xvi)   Retained earnings is one of the important long-term sources of finance for a new company.

(xvii)   Depreciation is a non-cash item.

(xviii) Dividend is an appropriation of profit.

(xix)   Dividend payout ratio is the ratio of cash dividend to net profits of the company.

(xx)   Dividend decision and dividend policy are same.

(xxi)   A 60% dividend payout ratio means 40% of the net profits are retained.

(xxii)   Share premium can be distributed as dividend.

(xxiii) Bonus can be issued in lieu of dividend.

(xxiv)   Declaration of cash dividend is likely to increase the market price of a share.

(xxv)   Dividend yield measures the dividend earning of a shareholder as a percentage of market price.

(II) Choose the appropriate answer:

(i)   Preference shares have _____
  (a) a preferential right as to dividend.
  (b) a preferential right as to repayment of capital in the event of company's winding-up.
  (c) a preferential right as to dividend and preferential right as to repayment of capital in the event of company winding-up.

(ii)   Interest payable on debentures is _____
  (a) an appropriation of profit.
  (b) a charge against profit.
  (c) a charge against sales revenues of the company.

(iii)   Trading on equity is possible _____
  (a) when capital structure of a company has fixed income bearing source of funds.
  (b) when the fixed interest rate is lower than the overall return on investment of the company.
  (c) when the capital structure of a company has fixed income bearing source of funds and the fixed interest rate is lower than the overall return on the company's investment.

(iv)   Zero coupon bonds carry _____
  (a) no interest.
  (b) no maturity value.
  (c) no charge against assets of the company.

(v)   Indenture is _____
  (a) a kind of debenture.
  (b) a legal agreement between company issuing debenture and the debenture trustee.
  (c) a agreement entered into between debenture holders and ordinary shareholders.

(vi)   Hybrid security is _____
  (a) Preference Shares.
  (b) Perpetual Debenture.
  (c) Sweat Equity Shares.

(vii)   Permanent working capital needs may be financed out of _____
    (a) long term sources.
    (b) issue of equity shares.
    (c) short-term loans.

(viii)   Internal sources of financing are less costly because _____
    (a) no floatation cost is involved
    (b) dividend rate on the increased capital is low
    (c) government gives tax concession to the companies using internal source of financing
    (d) all the above reasons

(ix)   Bonus issue can be made out of _____
    (a) General Reserve
    (b) Share Premium
    (c) Capital Reserve

(x)   Payout ratio means _____
    (a) payment made to the outsiders
    (b) dividend paid as a proportion to EPS
    (c) dividend paid
    (d) dividend on equity shares

(xi)   The permanent reduction in the value of Fixed Assets is _____
    (a) Depreciation
    (b) Depreciation Fund
    (c) Provision for Depreciation
    (d) Overhead

(xii)   Depreciation on Furniture is _____
    (a) Overhead
    (b) Administration Overhead
    (c) Direct Expenses
    (d) Production Overhead

(xiii)   Depreciation is recovered when _____
    (a) goods are sold for cash
    (b) tax is paid
    (c) asset is sold for replacement
    (d) none of the above

(xiv)   Trading on equity is possible only when _____
    (a) the capital structure of the company has fixed cost bearing funds
    (b) when company is financed out of equity funds only
    (c) when funds are raised through internal sources of finance
    (d) when a part of the profit is retained

(III) Differentiate between:
    (a) Ordinary shares and Preference shares.
    (b) Share and Debenture.
    (c) Term loan and Debenture.

(d) Rights and Sweat Equity Shares.

(e) Interest and Dividend.

(f) Public Deposits and Debentures.

(g) Cash Credit and Loan.

(h) Loan and Overdrafts.

(i) Cumulative and Participating Preference Shares.

(j) Floating charge and Fixed charge.

(k) Hypothecation and Pledge.

(l) Deep Discount Bonds and Issue of Bonds at a Discount.

(m) Internal Sources of Finance and External Sources of Finance

(n) Cash Dividend and Stock Dividend

(o) Final Dividend and Interim Dividend

(p) Preference Dividend and Equity Dividend

(q) Reserves and Provisions

(IV) Write short notes on:

(a) Premptive rights.

(b) Voting rights of Ordinary Shareholders.

(c) Deep Discount Bonds.

(d) Sweat Equity Shares.

(e) Covenants in case of Term Loans.

(f) Loan Syndication.

(g) Bridge Loan.

(h) Bonus shares

(i) Role of depreciation as an internal source of finance

(j) Ploughing back of profits

(V) Questions:

1. Examine the suitability of Term Loans for project financing.

2. Explain the sources of finance suitable for financing the purchase of fixed assets.

3. In what ways debenture issue is a better source of finance when compared to the 'issue of equity shares'.

4. "Stability of dividend is desirable for a company". Give reasons.

5. What are the factors influencing the dividend decision of a firm?

6. How is the growth of a company affected by the dividend decisions?

7. How are dividend decisions related to solvency of the company?

8. Explain the guidelines issued for 'Bonus issue' for SEBI.

9. What are the advantages of Bonus issue?

Questions from Previous Pune University Examinations

1. Limitations of Public Deposits.   **[April 2009, Oct. 2009]**

2. Write a short note on Dividend Policy.   **[April 2009, April 2010, Oct. 2011]**

3. What is meant by Debentures? Also explain its types with advantages and limitations.
         [April 2009, April 2010]

4. Write short note on Bonus Shares.   **[Oct. 2009, Oct. 2010]**
5. What are the different sources of External Financing? Also explain advantages and limitations of these sources.   **[Oct. 2009]**
6. Distinguish between Shares and Debentures.
                          [Oct. 2009, Oct. 2010, April 2012, Oct. 2012]
7. Write short note on Public Deposits.   **[Oct. 2010, April 2012, April 2013]**
8. Write short note Retained Earnings.   **[April 2011, Oct. 2012]**
9. Distinction between Internal Sources of Finance and External Sources of Finance.
                                                              [April 2011]
10. What are the different types of Shares? Explain their advantages and limitations.
                                                    [April 2011, Oct. 2012]
11. What is Dividend Policy? What are the various factors that determine Dividend Policy of a Company?   **[April 2011]**
12. Write short note Debentures.   **[Oct. 2011, Oct. 2012]**

13. Merits and demerits of Internal Sources of Finance.   **[Oct. 2011]**
14. What do you mean by Bonus Shares? What are the advantages of Bonus Shares? Explain the guidelines issued for 'Bonus Shares'.   **[Oct. 2011, April 2013]**
15. What are the various Internal Sources of Finance? Explain advantages and limitations of 'Reserves and Surplus' as one of the important Internal Sources of Finance.
                                                              [April 2012]
16. What are different types of Dividend Policy followed by the Companies? **[April 2012]**

17. Write short note on Demerits of Internal Source of Finance.   **[April 2013]**
18. What is Debenture? Explain types and merits of Debentures.   **[April 2013]**
                                                                    ■■■

Chapter 3...

Capital Structure

Contents ...

Learning Objectives:

➢ To understand the meaning of Capital, Capital Structure and Financial Structure
➢ To know the difference between levered and unlevered companies
➢ To get acquainted with trading on equity
➢ To understand capital structure decision
➢ To develop an understanding to the capital structure practices in India
➢ To define capitalisation and the theories of capitalisation
➢ To understand overcapitalisation and undercapitalisation and also comprehend the difference between the two.

3.1 Meaning of Capital

Capital refers to the money or money's worth contributed by the proprietors of a business and money contribution obtained from lenders for investing into business activities. The contribution of the owners is called the owned capital and the borrowings are called the debt capital. In case of a Joint Stock Company, the owner's contribution is called share capital and the borrowings are called as debt capital. Owner's funds or network includes, besides share capital, the undistributed profits or retained earnings.

Capital of a Joint Stock Company may consist of the following:

1. **Share Capital:**

   Ordinary/Equity Share Capital

   Preference Share Capital

2. **Reserves and Surplus:**

   Share Premium

   General Reserve

   Profit and Loss Account Balance

   Capital Reserves etc.

3. **Secured Loans:**

   Debentures

   Term Loans

Equity shareholders are the real owners of the company. They enjoy voting rights on the basis of proportionate voting share holdings. They are entitled to receive residual profit after tax, interest and preference dividend, provided Directors of the company declare the dividend.

Preference shareholders are entitled to get dividend at a fixed percentage of the nominal value of shares, before any dividend is paid to equity shareholders. These shareholders do not possess voting rights except when preference dividend has not been paid for a continuous period of 2 years. Share premium represents the excess of issue price over the face value of shares.

General Reserve is created out of the profits of the company by transferring some amount on a more or less regular basis.

Profit and Loss Account contains the profit balance left after the distribution of dividends if any and after transfer of reserves.

Capital Reserve is created out of such non-operating profits such as profit on re-issue of forfeited shares, profit made by holding company while acquiring shares in the subsidiary company.

Debenture is a form of borrowing by a company. The debenture holders are therefore, creditors to the company. It is mandatory for the company to pay interest at the fixed rate and to repay the principal amount, as agreed. The debenture holders do not have voting rights but their claims are secured by a floating or fixed charge on the assets of the company. In the event of non-payment by the company, they can take possession of the concerned asset and realise their dues.

Term loans are borrowed from the financial institutions for medium-term and long-term i.e. for a period beyond 5 years time. In the event of failure of the company, the financial institutions can nominate their Director in the Board of the company.

3.2 Capital Structure

The debt-equity mix of a firm is called capital structure. The long-term financing arrangements that a corporation has established is called the capital structure. It refers to the long-term financing mix of a company. A company can have any of the following capital structure:

(i)   Capital structure consisting of equity shares only;
(ii)   Equity share capital and Preference capital;
(iii)   Equity share capital and Debentures;
(iv)   Equity share capital, Preference share capital and Debentures;
(v)   Equity share capital, Reserves and Surpluses, Preference share capital, Debentures;
(vi)   Equity share capital, Reserves and Surpluses, Term loans and Debentures;
(vii)   Equity share capital, Reserves and Surplus and Term loans;
(viii) Equity share capital, Reserves and Surpluses and Preference share capital.

Companies may plan their capital structure or it may be the result of various financial decisions taken by the company over the years. Capital structure has a great impact on the overall earnings and earnings per share. It influences the liquidity and hence, solvency of a company.

3.3 Capital Structure and Financial Structure

Financial structure is broader when compared to capital structure. Financial structure refers to the way a firm's assets are financed, both fixed and current assets. It includes share capital, debt capital as well as short-term credit like: Creditors, Overdraft, Bills Payable etc. On the other hand, capital structure includes only the owners fund and long-term debts like Debentures, Term-loans etc.

3.4 Levered and Unlevered Companies

Use of fixed charges bearing funds in the capital structure of a company is called financial leverage. Preference share capital, Debenture and Term loans are fixed charge sources of funds. A company using these sources of funds is called a levered company. On the other hand, a company, which doesn't use either preference share capital or debt in its capital structure is called as an unlevered company.

Upto a certain level of earning i.e. EBIT (Earning Before Interest and Taxes) an unlevered company can pass on higher benefits to the equity shareholders and beyond the point of EBIT, it is a levered company which can provide higher EPS (Earnings Per Share). This point is called as 'indifference point'. The shareholders of a company would be indifferent to debt-equity mix, if the EBIT of the company is at this point. We can analyse the effect of change in capital structure with the help of the following example.

EBIT of the company is ₹ 8,00,000.

Tax rate applicable on the profits of the company – 35%.

Total capital of the company – ₹ 45,00,000.

Company has to decide a capital structure out of the four plans given below:

I Plan   :   Issue 45,000 shares of ₹ 100 each; or

II Plan   :   35,000 shares of ₹ 100 each and borrow ₹ 10,00,000 at 15% interest p.a.

III Plan   :   30,000 ordinary shares of ₹ 100 each and ₹ 15,00,000 through long-term borrowings at 16%.

IV Plan   :   35,000 ordinary shares of ₹ 100 each and ₹ 10,00,000 preference share capital with 14% dividend.

Let us calculate EPS which is, $\dfrac{\text{Net earnings available for equity shareholders}}{\text{Number of Equity shares}}$

Plans	I (₹)	II (₹)	III (₹)	IV (₹)
EBIT	8,00,000	8,00,000	8,00,000	8,00,000
Less: Interest p.a.	–	1,50,000	2,40,000	–
Earnings Before Tax (EBT)	8,00,000	6,50,000	5,60,000	8,00,000
Less: Tax @ 35%	2,80,000	2,27,500	1,96,000	2,80,000
Earnings After Tax (EAT)	5,20,000	4,22,500	3,64,000	5,20,000
Less: Preference Dividend	–	–	–	1,40,000
Earnings for Equity Shareholders	5,20,000	4,22,500	3,64,000	3,80,000
Number of Equity Shares	45,000	35,000	30,000	35,000
EPS	11.56	12.07	12.13	10.85

It may be observed that EPS is the highest in the III plan. Both the II and III plan make use of debt in the capital structure. Compared to all the equity plans and plan with equity and preference share capital, EPS is higher in the plans using debt. EPS is highest in case of III plan because it uses more amount of debt, although the rate of interest is higher.

It may further be noted that in the IV plan, the EPS is lowest despite the dividend rate being lower than the interest rates on debts. The reason being, interest on debt is tax deductible i.e., tax is paid on the profit left after the payment of interest. Hence, tax liability is less. On the other hand, preference dividend is not tax deductible, it is appropriation of profit after payment of tax. The tax liability in such a case is higher than when the debt is used.

3.5 Trading on Equity

A levered company can borrow money on the basis of the equity base. While borrowing, it will try to borrow such an amount on which the rate of interest is lower than the overall return on investment. After paying the interest, it can pass – on the remaining earnings in debt to the equity shareholders. This is called as Trading on equity. Trading on equity is more pronounced when debt is used, than when preference capital is used, because interest on debt is tax deductible whereas preference dividend is not tax deductible.

In the example given above, the overall return investment is,

$$ROI = \frac{EAT}{Capital\ employed} \times 100$$

$$= \frac{5,20,000}{45,00,000} \times 100$$

$$= 11.55\%$$

The interest expense on debt in the II plan is 15% whereas it is 16% in case of III plan. Both the rates of interest are lower than the return on investment. After paying the interest on debt, the remaining profit earned on the debt capital gets transferred to equity shareholders. Equity shareholders earning after tax is ₹ 5,20,000 on an investment of ₹ 45,00,000.

$$\text{The percentage of earnings} = \frac{5,20,000}{45,00,000} \times 100 = 11.55\%$$

When debt @ 16% is used the return to equity shareholders is 3,64,000 on an investment of ₹ 30,00,000.

$$\text{The percentage return on equity funds is} = \frac{3,64,000}{30,00,000} \times 100 = 12.13\%$$

Thus, due to the use of debt the % return on equity shareholders' funds has increased. This is called Trading on Equity or Financial Leverage.

3.6 Criteria for Determining Capital Structure

Financial manager needs to know the features of an appropriate capital structure. The following standards may be set to have best capital structure.

1. **Profitability**

   The most important criteria for determining appropriate capital structure is profitability. Profitability here means maximise the EPS and thereby improve the value of share and the firm. Profitability implies minimising cost of capital. Cost of capital to a firm is the minimum return which the suppliers of capital require.

2. **Solvency**

   Solvency is the financial state of a company or firm that is able to pay all debts as they fall due for payment. Firms may earn high return on their capital but may not have liquid assets to meet their financial obligations or to declare cash dividend. Even after earning profits, if a company fails to make payments of interest on borrowings, it may have to be closed for want of cash as the creditors may, as an extreme measure take hold of the secured asset and realise their dues. In the absence of these assets, it would be difficult for their firm to function.

   Capital structure should be designed in such a way that risk of insolvency is minimum. When companies make use of large amounts of debt, probably due to their incapacity to raise long-term funds through other sources, the cost of borrowing increases as lenders find it risky to lend to such firms. Besides excess use of debt may be perceived risky by equity shareholders and their requirement of return may also increase. Hence, the Financial Manager has to determine the right mix of debt and equity, by considering besides other things, the aspect of solvency.

3. **Flexibility**

   Flexibility is the ability to adapt an operating system to respond to changes in the environment. 'Flexibility' gives competitive advantage to a firm in a rapidly changing environment. It has two dimensions:

   (a) How quickly can an organisation change?

   (b) How far can it change?

   The capital structure should not be rigid. It must give room for changes, when change is desirable. Equity capital is not returned during the lifetime of the company. Equity share capital, hence, can provide, permanent capital to the company and its excessive use in the capital structure of a company might lead to inflexibility. On the other hand, use of redeemable preference share provides flexibility and at the same time doesn't threaten the solvency of the company. Term loans and Debentures are to be repaid after the stated time and hence, provide flexibility to the capital structure. But excessive use of debt might threaten the solvency of the firm.

   Flexibility means capacity to raise finance whenever it is required and capacity to redeem the capital whenever not required.

4. **Control**

   Control means to manage the business. A company may face dilution of control:

   (a) When more number of ordinary shares are issued to finance the long-term requirements of the firm, to the public.

   (b) When the company fails to pay preference dividend for a period of 2 years consecutively.

   (c) When it fails to pay the interest on its borrowing or to return the principal amount of debt as per the agreement.

   The appropriate capital structure is one which does not involve much risk of loss of control of the company.

   There is no best capital structure for all companies. It depends on the particular condition of business and may change from time to time. Financial Manager has to understand the environment and particular conditions of business while deciding about the capital structure of a company.

3.7 Capital Structure Decision

Capital structure decision is an ongoing work in a firm. The capital structure is planned initially when company is incorporated. The initial capital structure should be designed very carefully. While taking these decisions, the management must keep in view the overall objectives of the organisation in general and the financial management objective in particular. Company needs finance continuously and hence capital structure decisions are also continuous.

The determination of capital structure is a complicated task. It involves the consideration of a number of factors. There are three main approaches to capital structure decision:

1. Operating and Financial leverage.
2. Cost of capital.
3. Cash flow.

1. Financial leverage or Trading on Equity

The use of fixed cost sources of finance, such as debt and preference share capital to finance the assets of the company is known as Trading on Equity or Financial leverage. If the return on investment is higher than the interest rate on borrowing or preference dividend on preference capital, the EPS increases without increase in the owner's investment and without improvement in the operating efficiency of the firm.

Financial leverage is one of the most important considerations of capital structure decision as it affects the EPS. All firms cannot make profitable use of financial leverage. A company with high level of earnings before interest and taxes (EBIT) can make use of high degree of leverage. Companies with low EBIT and companies under unfavourable conditions may find that the rate of return on total assets is less than the cost of debt, the EPS will fall with the degree of leverage. It can be proved with the following illustration:

Suppose a company wants to make a total investment of ₹ 5,00,000. Following are the other details.

Plans	EBIT	Tax Rate
I. All equity shares of ₹ 100 each	I. 2,50,000	50%
	II. 75,000	
II. ₹ 3,00,000 in equity shares and ₹ 2,00,000 brings at 18%.		

We can analyse the relationship between EBIT-EPS under two different plans, at two different EBIT levels.

(A) When EBIT is ₹ 2,50,000:

	Plan I	Plan II
EBIT	2,50,000	2,50,000
Less: Interest	–	36,000
EBT	2,50,000	2,14,000
Less: Tax @ 50%	1,25,000	1,07,000
EAT/Income available to equity shareholders	1,25,000	1,07,000
EPS	₹ 25	₹ 35.67

$$\text{Company's ROI} = \frac{2,50,000 - 1,25,000}{5,00,000} \times 100$$

$$= 25\%$$

But the rate of interest payable on borrowings is 18%. Thus, it can be proved that when the companies EBIT is very high, it can make use of debt capital, where cost is less than its overall earning percentage and can increase EPS.

(B) When EBIT is ₹ 75,000:

	Plan I	Plan II
EBIT	75,000	75,000
Less: Interest	–	36,000
EBT	75,000	39,000
Less: Tax @ 50%	37,500	19,500
EAT	37,500	19,500
EPS	7.5	6.5

It can be observed that when EBIT is ₹ 75,000 the EPS is less in the II plan where debt has been used.

The ROI of the company is $= \dfrac{37,500}{5,00,000} \times 100 = 7.5\%$

Company's ROI is much less than the rate of interest on borrowings which is 18%. Hence, company cannot use financial leverage to the advantage of its shareholders. There is a point of EBIT where EPS is same, irrespective of whether debt is used or not. Such a point is called Break-even point. If EBIT earned by the company is less than the break-even point, the company should not use fixed cost sources of finance. On the other hand, if the EBIT level is more than the break-even point, a company can use debt capital or preference capital to increase the EPS. Break-even point can be shown by way of a graph as shown below.

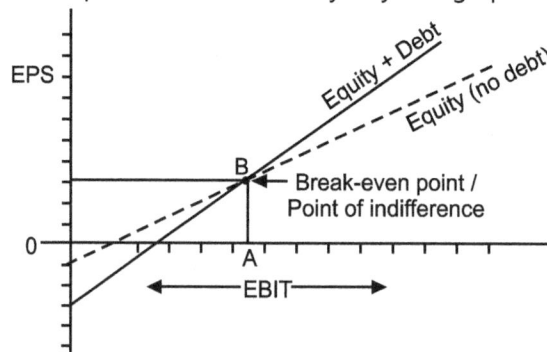

Fig. 3.1: Graphical Representation of the Break-even Point

At point B, which is also known as indifference point, the EPS will remain the same irrespective of whether company uses debt or not. It may be noted that when EBIT is less than that at point A, EPS is higher by using no debt in the capital structure. Whereas, when EBIT is more than that at point A, EPS is higher with the use of EBIT.

2. Cost of Capital Approach

Cost of capital refers to the rate of return expected by the suppliers of finance. Each source has its own cost. For example, the cost of borrowing is the rate of interest minus the tax advantage cost of preference share is the preference dividend, floatation cost and premium if any payable on redemption etc. Financial Manager may have to consider the impact of overall cost of capital on the value of the firm rather than considering the cost of each component of capital structure in isolation. This is because, change in debt has an impact on the risk of equity shareholders and hence their expected return. When debt component in the capital structure increases, the risk of the lenders increases and hence, beyond a certain point, the lenders would demand higher rate of interest. As the debt component increases, the risk of the ordinary shareholders also increase, who in turn expect higher rate of return. Thus, cost of equity capital also increases. The overall cost of capital also increases with the increase in cost of both the component capitals. The value of the firm decreases with an increase in cost. An optimum capital structure minimises the cost of capital lending to maximising value of the firm. EBIT remaining the same, an increase in the overall cost of capital reduces the value of the firm and a decrease in the cost of capital will increase the overall cost of capital.

3. Liquidity consideration / Approach (Cash Flow Analysis)

This approach considers liquidity as an important consideration for determining capital structure. The capital structure should be designed in such a way that the firm doesn't have to face liquidity crisis, i.e. shortage of cash to meet various obligations. Besides, it should supply minimum required cash even in times of adverse situations (low market demand).

Some cash flows are obligatory like interest and principle amount whereas some others are discretionary like dividend payment. In times of liquidity crisis, company can avoid making dividend payment but not interest payment. Hence, if a firm expects to earn non-uniform profits, it may have to keep its debt proportion very low and try to trade on equity by using preference capital. On the other hand, if future cash outflows are expected to be uniform, then a firm could use debt to take advantage of trading on equity without being threatened by insolvency.

4. Control

Capital structure decision is guided by the extent of control the management and shareholders want to retain. Issue of preference shares and debentures and borrowing term loans doesn't interfere with the existing control by equity shareholders as the providers of capital do not possess any voting rights. But if company fails to meet its obligations, control may get diluted. Issue of equity share dilutes control of existing shareholders as equity shares, carry voting rights.

5. Marketability

Marketability means the capacity of the firm to sell its securities such as shares and debentures to the investors. It is the readiness of investors to purchase a security in a given period of time at a reasonable return. The capital markets are changing continuously. Sometimes, equity shares are demanded and other times debentures are readily bought. A firm must consider not only the internal conditions but also general market conditions. When share market is at its low, company should not issue common shares but issue debt.

6. Floatation Costs

Floatation cost refers to the cost incurred when funds are externally raised. The cost of floating debt is generally less than the cost of floating shares. Use of retained earnings doesn't involve any floatation cost. These costs are not an important factor for determining capital structure, but they do affect the size of money raised through various issues. The costs tend to decline with larger amount of funds.

7. Size of the company

A small size company may find it difficult to raise fund. On the other hand, it is easy for large size firms to obtain loan or issue shares and debentures. Small size companies may find that the restrictive convenants in the long-term loan agreements, have made the capital structure very inflexible. Issue of further share dilute control as their shares are not widely sold/bought.

8. Period of Finance

The period for which finance is required also affects the determination of capital structure of companies. For less than 3 years, public deposits or short-term loans from banks may be an appropriate source of funds. On the other hand, if finance is required for a long period beyond 5 years time debentures, redeemable preference shares, or term loans may be best options. On the other hand, for permanent capital requirements issue of equity shares may be apt.

9. Purpose of Financing

The capital structure or changes in the capital structure are determined by the purpose for which funds are required. For example, for purchase of machine, issue of debenture or term loan may be better, as the profit generated by this productive asset can be used to pay interest as well as to repay the principle amount. On the other hand, when purpose of raising finance is 'unproductive in nature', such as welfare expenditure for the employees in the form of contribution of school, hospital etc. can be financed by the issue of equity shares.

10. Government Policy

Government policy is also an important factor in planning the company's capital structure. For example, a change in the lending policy of financial institution on the basis of the monetary policy adopted by the Government, may change the availability of loan and rate of interest.

11. Nature of Industry

The nature of industry is one of the most important elements in determining the debt-equity ratio. If the sales of an industry show lot of fluctuations, the company should use low leverage since the risk of non-payment of interest may cause problems of insolvency. On the other hand, if industry faces a high degree of steady sales, the debt-equity ratio can be high, i.e. company can use financial leverage.

12. Tax Planning

Tax planning is likely to have a significant bearing on capital structure decisions. The interest on borrowed funds is allowed as a deduction under the Income Tax Act, 1961; while dividend on shares is not deductible from the operating profits of a company.

A host of factors influence the determination of capital structure of a company. Some of these factors are conflicting in nature. The management of a company will have to evolve the optimum capital structure considering these factors, by assigning weightage to different factors on the basis of the particular facts of the case.

3.8 Capital Structure Practices in India

The capital structure practices in India have the following features:

1. Indian companies use substantial amount of debt in their capital structures in terms of debt-equity ratio as well as total debt to total assets ratio.
2. Companies prefer long-term borrowing to short-term borrowing.
3. Due to use of debt, Indian companies are exposed to a high degree of risk.
4. The debt service capacity of the a large segment of corporate borrowers is inadequate and unsatisfactory.
5. Retained earnings are the most favoured source of finance.
6. The hybrid securities are the least popular source of finance.
7. Equity capital as a source of funds is not preferred across the board.

3.9 Meaning of Capitalisation

Capital refers to the sum total of long-term funds invested in the assets of the company including equity share capital, preference share capital, debentures and long-term fund. Capitalisation in common parlance is the act of providing capital for a company or other organisations.

According to **Dewing**, "*Capitalisation includes capital stock and debt*". Capitalisation, therefore includes shares and debentures issued by the company and also the long-term loans taken from financial institutions.

3.10 Definitions of Capitalisation

1. According to **Gerstenburg**, *"Capitalisation comprises of a company's ownership capital which include capital stock and surplus in whatever form it may appear and borrowed capital which consists of bonds or similar evidence of long-term debt".*

2. **Bonneville** and **Deway** define, *" Capitalisation is the balance sheet values of stocks and bonds outstanding".*

3. According to **Walker** and **Baughn**, *"Capitalisation refers only to long-term debt and capital stock and short-term creditors do not constitute suppliers of capital. In reality total capital is furnished by short-term creditors and long-term creditors".*

4. According to **Guthmann** and **Dougall**, *"Capitalisation is the sum of the par value of the outstanding stocks and bonds".*

It can be observed from the above mentioned definitions that there is no unanimity of opinion among the authors regarding the concept of capitalisation. These definitions can be divided into two categories: Broad interpretation and Narrow interpretation.

3.10.1 Broad Interpretation

In the broad sense capitalisation is the act of determining the total requirement of finance in the company as well as the determination of the capital mix i.e. the proportion of equity, preference, debenture and term loan in the capital structure of the company. In other words, it not only includes the quantity of capital but also the quality of capital.

3.10.2 Narrow Interpretation

As per the narrow interpretation, the term capitalisation includes only the determination of the amount of long-term funds in the business. The decision about the mix of capital is capital structure decisions.

3.10.3 Some other Interpretations of the term Capitalisation

The term capitalisation can also be interpreted as:

1. Conversion of the retained earnings of the company by issue of Bonus shares i.e. ploughing back of profits.

2. The accounting practice of treating an expenditure as asset rather than charging it to profit and loss account.

Capitalisation thus refers to the long-term indebtedness and includes both the ownership and the borrowed capital. Capital and Capitalisation are two different terms. The term 'capitalisation' is used only in relation to companies and not in respect of partnership firms or sole proprietorships. It is distinguished from 'capital' which represents total investment or resources of a company. It thus represents total wealth of the company. Capitalisation means the total par value of all the securities, i.e. shares and debentures issued by a company and reserves, surplus and value of all other long-term obligations.

3.11 Theories of Capitalisation

The theories of capitalisation guide a new company in determining the quality of investment:

1. **Cost Theory**

   This theory helps in determining the total investment required in establishing the business. The total investment consists of the total finance required for acquiring:

   1. Fixed assets like land, building, machinery etc.

   2. Working capital amount – The part of the capital required for carrying day-to-day trading operations. It consists of current assets such as stock, debtors, cash etc. less current liabilities viz. trade creditors.

   3. The cost of establishing the business such as cost of floatation of shares and debentures, preliminary expenses etc.

   As per the cost theory, capitalisation is the sum total of all the costs incurred to acquire assets etc. But if the cost of asset does not match with the worth of the asset in the sense. If the assets generate less profit than that expected, there may be over-capitalisation. Thus, this theory fails to consider the earning capital of the investment.

2. **Earnings Theory**

   This theory emphasises the earning capacity of a business. Earning is the basis of capitalisation. Thus, according to this theory earnings are capitalised at a representative rate of return. This method involves the following steps:

   (a) **Determination of future earnings:** A number of factors are considered for determining the future earnings of the company such as firms capacity and capacity utilisation, market demand and share in the total market demand, non-recurring factors, state of the economy, government policy etc. since there is uncertainty involved, lot of precaution is required to be taken while estimating future returns. More than one estimation can be made and weighted average of the returns may be found out.

   (b) **Determination of capitalisation rate:** Capitalisation rate can be the cost of capital i.e. the expected rate of return of the investors, rate of earnings of similar firm in the same industry, etc.

   (c) **Capitalise the returns at the rate determined.**

   Amount of capitalisation can be found out by applying the following formula:

   $$\frac{\text{Future expected earnings}}{\text{Capitalisation rate}} \times 100$$

   The earnings theory of capitalisation is considered as the best method for existing companies, and cost method is considered suitable for a new company.

3.12 Overcapitalisation

Overcapitalisation is a condition in which an organisation has too much capital for the needs of the business. In such a situation a company is likely to be overburdened by interest charged by the need to spread profits by way of dividend. It is a situation where the earnings on the total capital employed is less than the normal rate of return expected. It also means that the real value of total assets is less than the book value of the total assets. Overcapitalisation is an indication that the existing capital has not been effectively utilised resulting in fall in the earnings. Thus, overcapitalisation is a relative term. Capital in relation to earnings is what measures overcapitalisation.

3.12.1 Definition

According to **Gerstenburg**, "A corporation is overcapitalised when its earnings are not large enough to yield a fair return on the amount of stocks and bonds that have been issued or when the amount of securities outstanding exceeds the current value of assets".

A firm is said to be overcapitalised when:

(a) a fair return cannot be obtained on capitalisation;

(b) capitalisation exceeds the real economic value of its net assets.

(c) assets available with the business are more then what are needed.

3.12.2 Overcapitalisation Vs Excess Capital

Overcapitalisation doesn't mean excess capital. Overcapitalisation is a relative term, which measures the earnings with that of the capital employed. It may be an indication of the existence of idle or obsolete capital.

For example: A company earns ₹ 3,00,000 on a total capital investment of ₹ 30,00,000. If the return expected is 10%, than the business is said to be properly capitalised. On the other hand if the return expected is 12% i.e. ₹ 3,60,000, then the company would be said to be ovecapitalised.

This can be explained with the help of the following illustration:

Balance Sheet

Share Capital @ ₹ 10	2,50,000	Assets	4,00,000
Reserves	50,000		
Term loan	75,000		
Sundry Creditors	25,000		
	4,00,000		**4,00,000**

Let the capitalisation or the normal rate of earning by 15%. The net earnings of the company be ₹ 20,000.

1. Capital invested in the business is

	2,50,000
	+ 50,000
	+ 75,000
	3,75,000

2. Net earnings → ₹ 1,000.

3. Capitalised value of earnings is ₹ $\dfrac{20,000 \times 100}{15} = 1,33,333.$

Conclusions:

1. On the investment company should have earned @15% of ₹ 56,250. But the earnings of the company is low. Hence, the company is overcapitalised.

2. Further as per the capitalisation of earnings the required capital is only ₹ 1,33,333, whereas the actual investment in the business is ₹ 3,75,000.

3. The book value of equity capital is $\dfrac{3,00,000}{25,000} = ₹ 12.$

whereas the real value of an equity share is $\dfrac{1,33,000}{25,000} = 5.33$ per share.

3.12.3 Causes of Overcapitalisation

1. **Inaccurate estimation of earnings:** The earning capitalisation method makes use of future expected net earnings and expected rate of return to compute the quantity of capitalisation. The estimation of future earnings is a difficult task due to the uncertainty present in the market. If the estimation is inaccurate, the capital requirement calculated on the basis of erroneous estimation is bound to be incorrect. Overcapitalisation results when future expected earnings is estimated at a higher level than the actual earnings.

2. **Overvaluation of assets:** The book value of assets shown in the Balance Sheet is more than the real value of assets. This can happen in the following situations:

   (a) **Inadequate depreciation:** If the fixed assets have not been sufficiently depreciated, the asset may be overstated in the Balance Sheet. The company may not have judged properly the wear and tear in the assets, or else the method of depreciation adopted by the company may be inaccurate.

   (b) **Vendor company is paid higher consideration:** When a partnership firm is converted into a company, the company might have paid more amount of purchase consideration than the real worth of the assets. The value placed on the asset, while taking over, may not be on the basis of the earning capacity of the assets. Overvaluation of asset results in overcapitalisation.

3. **Wrong estimation of the capitalisation rate:** Determination of the capitalisation rate is a very important step in the determination of capitalisation. If the capitalisation rate is estimated at a figure lower than the actual rate, it would result in over capitalisation. If the earnings are capitalised at a lower rate than the actual rate, capitalised amount would be higher. Thus, the estimated capital of the company would be more than what it should be. Hence, there may be a situation of overcapitalisation.

4. **Faulty Financial Plan:** Improper financial planning may lead to lack of capital. The shortage of capital may be made good by resorting to costlier sources of finance. These kind of financial decisions may result in an unnecessary high cost of debt service leading to reduction in the earnings of the shareholders. This will lead to reduction in the value of shares. One of the indicators of overcapitalisation is when the real value of shares is less than the book value.

5. **Market conditions:** When the capital market is favourable, a company might raise huge funds to make use of the convenient and less costly capital. But if this huge finance could not be used by the firm due to non-availability of opportunities for profitable investment, or it uses the funds in low earnings securities of the Government, the overall return on capital invested would fall and there would be overcapitalisation.

6. **Improper plan for replacement of asset:** A firm must start providing for replacement of an asset, when an asset is purchased. If it doesn't create provision or sinking fund for its replacement, it might find it tough to arrange for the purchase of a new fixed asset in place of the old, form cash generated out of operations. In such a situation the company might be forced to borrow at a high rate of interest resulting in low returns of overcapitalisation.

7. **Inflationary conditions:** If assets are bought during inflation, the total value placed on the asset may be more than its real worth. During rising prices firms pay for goods and services at higher prices than they are worth. As a result the return on investment declines leading to overcapitalisation.

8. **Improper dividend policy:** When a company follows a liberal policy of paying cash dividends without creating reserves and without planning cash flows properly, the funds deplete and the company may resent borrowing to repay its sold debts. This may lead to reduction in net earnings and also overcapitalisation.

9. **Taxation policy:** If a firm does not plan its tax properly, it may land up paying huge amounts of taxes, depleting the funds needed of renewal and replacement of assets. The efficiency of the assets would get adversely affected ultimately decreasing the value of the asset.

10. **Existence of absolute asset:** If the assets include unused and obsolete (outdated) assets overcapitalisation may occur.

3.12.4 Consequences of Overcapitalisation

Overcapitalisation has the following evil effects:

1. Return on investment is low in situations of overcapitalisation. After payment of interest and taxes out of the low earnings what is left is meant for equity shareholders. The EPS falls and hence there is a considerable reduction in the **rate of dividend** on equity shares.

2. Due to fall in EPS and fall in the real value of shares of the company, shareholders lose confidence in the company. Consequently, the **market price** of the share falls. This reduces the prospects of capital gain to the shareholders.

3. In order to hide their inefficiency the Board of Directors may resort to **window-dressing** by various means.

4. The company may have to go in for internal re-organisation or else may have to resort to **liquidation**.

3.12.5 Remedies for Overcapitalisation

1. **Internal Reconstruction:** A company may have to go in for a reorganisation of capital structure. This is also known as 'Capital reduction' since the equity shareholders, debenture holders, lenders and creditors may be asked to reduce their claim in the assets of the company. The amount so saved would be used to write off all accumulated losses, goodwill and obsolete assets. In order to convince these suppliers of finance to agree for a lesser claim, the company might offer a higher rate of interest of preference dividend.

2. **Repayment of loan or debts:** If the company doesn't have problems of shortage of cash, it may repay its long-term debts, thereby reducing the idle cash on one hand and the idle capital on the other hand. The repayment of loan and debt would increase the net earnings of the company due to the absence of interest payment. The rate of return on capital would rise, partly due to reduction in total capital and partly due to increase in net earnings.

3. **Buy-back shares:** A company can buy-back its own shares for restructuring of its capital. Buy-back reduces the retained profits (part of owner's capital) on one hand and cash on the other hand. It reduces the share capital of the company. Total capital reduces, leading to increase in the rate of earnings on capital invested.

3.13 Undercapitalisation

Undercapitalisation is the state of the company that does not have sufficient capital or reserve for the size of its operations. A growing company might find that such a company is making profits but is unable to convert these profits quickly into cash to pay its debts. Under capitalisation is said to exist when:

1. the rate of earnings are much higher than the normally expected rate of returns.

2. the increase in the market value of shares is much more than other similar companies.

According to **Gerstenburg**, "A corporation may be under capitalised when the rate profit is exceptionally high in relation to the return enjoyed by similar suitable companies in the same industry. The assets may be worth more than the values reflected in the books.

Undercapitalisation is the reverse of overcapitalisation. It does not imply shortage of funds. It means that the company is earning more than what is normally expected on similar capital employed in the given circumstances. When compared to the earnings the capital investment is low.

3.13.1 Causes of Undercapitalisation

1. **Conservative Estimate of Earning:** Initially, while computing the future earnings, the company might have made very conservative estimates. This leads to lower capitalisation, thus leading to undercapitalisation.

2. **Use of High Capitalisation rate:** While determining capitalisation, a high capitalisation rate might have been used resulting in low capital and then to undercapitalisation.

3. **Setting-up during recession:** Recession is a period of slow down in the economy. Prices tend to fall. If a company was set up during recession it would have purchased the assets at low prices. Such a company becomes undercapitalised after recession is over, due to the purchase of assets at exceptionally low prices and due to a low capitalisation rate. As soon as the recession is over, the earning capacity of the company increases which results in increasing the real value of the assets of the company.

4. **Conservative dividend policy:** Conservative dividend policy means a company has been paying very low cash dividends leading to building up of internal sources of finance for expansion. This improves the earning capacity of the company.

5. **Efficiency:** The management in a company might have been very efficient in operations. There might have been optimum utilisation of every asset, labour and management time. This might have resulted in a high rate of return on investment.

6. **Excessive Provision for depreciation:** If depreciation is provided in excess of the requirements, there would be creation of secret reserves and the real value of the asset would be more than their book values. This would result in undercapitalisation.

3.13.2 Consequences of Undercapitalisation

1. Encouraged by the high earnings, **new entrepreneurs** would enter the same industry which might make the competition very intense.

2. **Labour might** be dissatisfied that the benefits of their efficiency is not passed on to them. This would create unnecessary labour unrest.

3. **Consumers** might feel exploited. They might feel that the company is making high profits by charging a high price from them.

4. Government may interfere to safeguard the interest of the dissatisfied consumers, employees and investors etc.

5. Higher earnings would make the company bear the heavy burden of taxation.

6. The market price of the share may become very high which may bring restrictions on its marketability.

3.13.3 Remedial Measures

1. **Issue of bonus shares:** This is the best method usually followed for correcting undercapitalised situation. This would result in increasing the number of shares, although total capitalisation remains the same. But this has the effect of reducing the EPS.

2. **Increasing par value of shares:** Par value of shares might be increased. This will bring down the percentage of equity earnings although earnings per share may not reduce.

3. **Increasing the number of shares:** Number of shares might be increased by stock split up. This would increase the number of shares and therefore would decrease the earnings per share.

3.14 Overcapitalisation Vs Undercapitalisation

Both overcapitalisation and undercapitalisation are harmful to the firm.

However, if observed carefully, one will find that the effects of overcapitalisation are more serious. It hurts and affects the company, shareholders, consumers and society. It can result in liquidation and winding-up off the company, which can be a very high cost to pay for the company.

Undercapitalisation on the other hand increases congestion for the company, leads to discontentment among the employees and the consumers feel exploited.

The harmful effects may be compared as follows:

1. In case of overcapitalisation earnings decline and much of the investment is idle or underutilised.

   On the other hand in case of undercapitalisation, the rate of earnings is high, but once the new entrepreneurs enter the field, much of the market share and earnings might be snatched away by the competitions.

2. Overcapitalisation might have taken place due to the existence of fictitious and worthless assets. On the other hand in undercapitalisation, the real value of the assets is much more than what is stated in the books.

3. In case of overcapitalisation there might be retrenchment of employees, whereas in case of undercapitalisation there might be labour unrest.

4. It is easy to correct undercapitalisation than overcapitalisation.

Undercapitalisation is a lesser evil when compared to overcapitalisation.

Points to Remember

- **Capital** refers to the money or money's worth contributed by the proprietors of a business and money contribution obtained from lenders for investing into business activities. The contribution of the owners is called the owned capital and the borrowings are called the debt capital.

- **Capital Structure:** A company can have the following capital structures:
    (i)   Capital structure consisting of equity shares only
    (ii) Equity share capital and preference capital
    (iii) Equity share capital and debentures
    (iv) Equity share capital, preference share capital and debentures
    (v)   Equity share capital, reserves and surpluses, term loans and debentures
    (vi) Equity share capital, reserves and surpluses, and term loans
    (vii) Equity share capital, reserves and surpluses, term loans and debentures
    (viii) Equity share capital, reserves and surpluses and preference share capital

- **Levered and Unlevered Companies:** A company using sources of funds is called a levered company. A company which doesn't use either preference share capital or debt in its capital structure is called an unlevered company.

- **Criteria for determining capital structure:**
    (i)   Profitability
    (ii) Solvency
    (iii) Flexibility
    (iv) Control

- **Three main approaches to capital structure decision are:** Operating and financial leverage, Cost of capital, Cash flow, **Others include:** Control, Marketability, Floatation Costs, Size of company, Period of Finance, Purpose of financing, Government Policy, Nature of Industry, Tax Planning.

- **Capitalisation** is the balance sheet values of stocks and bonds outstanding.

- **Theories of capitalistaion:**
    (i)   Cost Theory
    (ii) Earnings Theory

- A firm is said to be **overcapitalised** when:
    (i)   A fair return cannot be obtained on capitalisation
    (ii) Capitalisation exceeds the real economic value of its net assets
    (iii) Assets available with the business are more than what are needed

- **Undercapitalisation** is said to exist when:
    (i)   The rate of earnings are much higher than the normally expected rate of returns
    (ii) The increase in the market value of shares is much more than other similar companies

Questions for Discussion

I.   State whether the following statements are True or False:

(i)   The term 'Capital structure' includes 'Financial structure' also.

(ii)   Optimum Capital structure is obtained when the market value of the firm is maximised and cost is minimised.

(iii)   The value of a levered firm is always more than that of an unlevered firm.

(iv)   If the EBIT is below the indifference point, a company should use owned funds to maximise EPS.

(v)   Preference dividend is tax deductible.

(vi)   Capital structure refers to the debt-equity ratio.

(vii)   Capital and Capitalisation mean the same.

(viii) Overvaluation of assets leads to undercapitalisation.

(ix)   Insufficient depreciation earns overcapitalisation.

(x)   Overcapitalisation means excess capital.

(xi)   A company which is set-up during recession may suffer from overcapitalisation, after the recovery.

II. Questions:

1.   Explain the term 'Point of Indifference'.

2.   What is optimum capital structure?

3.   Explain the factors that determine the capital structure of a firm.

4.   Explain the cost theory approach to capital structure determination.

5.   Explain the EBIT-EPS approach for determining the capital structure of a firm.

6.   What are the criteria of appropriate capital structure?

7.   What are the causes of overcapitalisation? How can it be corrected?

8.   Compare overcapitalisation and undercapitalisation.

9.   What are the causes of undercapitalisation? What are the remedial measures?

10. Analyse the impact of the state of economy on capitalisation.

Questions from Previous Pune University Examinations

1. Write short note Trading in Equity.   **[April 2009]**

2. Write short note factors influencing Capital Structure.   **[April 2009]**

3. What is Overcapitalisation? Also explain causes, consequences and remedies of Overcapitalisation.   **[April 2009, April 2013]**

4. Explain meaning of Capital Structure and also explain in detail criteria for determining Capital Structure.   **[April 2009, April 2010]**

5. Write short note on Capitalisation.   **[Oct. 2009]**

6. Write short note Consequences of Overcapitalisation.   **[Oct. 2009]**

7. What do you understand by Owned capital and Borrowed Capital? Also explain different types of Debentures in detail.   **[Oct. 2009]**

8. What do you mean by Capital Structure? What different criteria should be considered in determining Capital Structure?   **[Oct. 2009, April 2013]**

9. Write short note on Trading in equity.   **[April 2010]**

10. Write short note on Capitalisation.   **[April 2010]**

11. What is Undercapitalisation? What are its effects? Also explain various remedies available for Undercapitalisation.   **[April 2010]**

12. Write short note Trading in Equity.   **[Oct. 2010, April 2013]**

13. What is Over capitalisation? Explain in detail the effects and remedies of Over capitalisation.   **[Oct. 2010]**

14. What is 'Capital Structure'? Explain in detail factors influencing Capital Structure.

                                                                          [Oct. 2010]

15. Write short note Under-capitalisation.   **[April 2011]**

16. What do you mean by Capital Structure? Explain in detail various factors influencing Capital Structure.   **[April 2011]**

17. What is Over-capitalisation? What are the causes, consequences and remedies of Over-capitalisation?   **[April 2011]**

18. Write short note on Capitalisation.   **[Oct. 2011, Oct. 2012]**

19. What do you mean by Capital Structure? What are the factors influencing the Composition of Capital Structure?   **[Oct. 2011]**

20. "As between Under and Over-capitalisation, the former is the lesser evil of the two but still both should be discouraged and the ideal should be fair capitalisation". Comment.

                                                                          [Oct. 2011]

21. Write short note Overcapitalisation.   **[April 2012]**

22. Write short note on Factors Influencing Capital Structure.   **[April 2012]**

23. What do you mean by Capital Structure? What are the factors that influence the composition of Capital Structure.   **[Oct. 2012]**

24. What is Undercapitalisation? Explain the causes of Undercapitalisation. What are the remedial measures?   **[Oct. 2012]**

■■■

Chapter 4...

Financial Planning

Contents ...

Learning Objectives:

➢ To understand the meaning, definition and objectives of financial planning

➢ To study the principles of a good financial plan

➢ To know the types of financial plans

➢ To comprehend the areas and steps of financial planning

➢ To grasp the significance of financial planning

➢ To study the methods of forecasting

Introduction

Planning is a process involving the determination of a future course of action. Planning helps an organisation to be focused on its goals. It provides alternative courses of action when situations change. It guides the organisation, as planning is concerned with looking into the future and the selection of the most suitable course of action.

4.1 Meaning and Definitions of Financial Planning

Financial planning involves planning the financial operations in advance so as to help in achieving the objectives of the enterprise. Financial operations consist of:

1. Procurement of finance at the right time, when it is needed and;
2. Effective utilisation of finance.

According to **Walker and Boughn**, *"Financial planning pertains to the function of finance and includes the determination of the firm's financial objectives, formulating and promulgating financial policies and developing financial procedures".*

According to **P. V. Kulkarni,** *"Planning is essentially concerned with the economical procurement and profitable use of funds – a use which is determined by realistic investment decisions".*

According to the **Oxford Dictionary of Business and Management**, *"Financial planning is the formulation of short-term and long-term plans in financial terms for the purpose of establishing goals for an organisation to achieve, against which its actual performance can be measured".*

From the above definitions, following features of Financial planning can be derived:

1. Financial planning is related to financial operations of a business viz., procurement of finance and its use for various purposes of the organisation.
2. Financial planning is concerned with both the short-term and the long-term financial plan. In other words, planning for finance includes working capital planning as well as planning for capital of a firm.
3. It determines the financial objectives of a firm.
4. It includes formulation of procedures and policies for the financial operations of the business.
5. It aims at procuring the finance from the right source at minimum costs, when needed.
6. It helps in making profitable use of the funds acquired.
7. Financial planning is an ongoing process as finance is required at every stage in the life of a business. It is an important consideration for growth, expansion, dividend declaration, credit period decisions, investment decisions etc.

4.2 Objectives of Financial Planning

In the opinion of **Cohen** and **Robbins**, financial planning should:

(i)   Determine the *financial resources* required to meet the company's operating programme.

(ii) Forecast the extent to which these requirements will be met by internal generation of funds and to what extent they will be met by external sources.

(iii) Develop the *best plans* and to obtain the requirement of external funds.

(iv) Establish and maintain a *system of financial controls* governing the allocation and use of funds.

(v)   *Formulate programmes* to provide the most effective profit-volume-cost relationships.

(vi) *Report* the facts to the top management and make recommendations on future operations of the firm.

4.3 Principles of a Good Financial Plan - Basic Considerations

A financial plan should be made, ensuring that the following principles are incorporated in it:

1. **Simplicity:** The financial plan should be simple to understand and easy to follow. It should provide for minimum types of securities for raising finance.

2. **Flexibility:** A business operates in a dynamic and uncertain environment. Even the best method of forecasting events may not be accurate. Hence, the plan must provide room for flexibility, in the sense it must be possible to change the plan when situations change.

3. **Liquidity:** *Liquid assets*, refer to the assets held in cash or in any other form that can be easily turned into cash with minimum loss. Example, Bank Current Account Deposits, Trade Debtors, Marketable Investment etc. *Liquidity* is the extent to which an organisation's assets are liquid, enabling it to pay its debts when they fall due for payment and also to move into new investment opportunities.

    The financial plan must provide for sufficient liquidity to the business, so that obligations can be met in time, and opportunities of further investment is not lost due to lack of liquidity.

4. **Optimum Use:** Financial plan should make available the needed finance at the right time, in the right amount, so that the funds are neither kept idle, nor there is paucity of funds. Idle funds may lead to over capitalisation.

5. **Cost:** Financial plan should help procure right amount of finance at the minimum cost, so that profitability is enhanced.

6. **Co-ordination of long-term and short-term financial plan:** Short-term plan and long-term plan must be co-ordinated. The dividend decision should not be in conflict with long-term growth objectives of the company.

4.4 Types of Financial Plans

Financial plans can be short-term and long-term. Short-term plans are for a period of time, less than one year, and are called Budgets. Whereas, long-term plans are meant for more than one year, like capital budgeting.

4.4.1 Budget

Budget is a financial or quantitative statement, prepared prior to a specified accounting period, containing the plans and policies to be pursued during the budget period. Generally, a functional budget is drawn up for each functional area within an organisation. In addition a 'capital budget', consisting of a cash flow budget, stock budget and a master budget is prepared. It includes the preparation of Budgeted Profit and Loss Account.

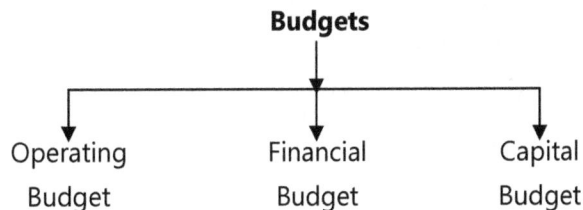

Budgets

| Operating | Financial | Capital |
| Budget | Budget | Budget |

4.4.2 Operating Budgets

Operating Budgets relate to the planning of the activities of the business enterprise, such as production, sales and purchases. It consists of programme budget and responsibility budget. A programme or activity budget specifies the operations or functions to be performed during the next year. Responsibility budget specifies the plans in terms of individual responsibility. The focus is on individuals.

Operating budget can be prepared for a period and no change will be introduced in the plan during the period of its implementation. Another way to prepare an operating budget is, to prepare continuous budget that makes changes or revise the plans as per the changed conditions.

4.4.3 Financial Budgets

These budgets are concerned with the financial implications of the operating budgets. It analyses the cash inflows and outflows, financial position and the operating results.

It includes:

- Cash Budget
- Proforma Financial Statements.

4.4.4 Capital Budget

It involves the planning to acquire worthwhile projects together with the timings of the estimated cost and cash flows of each project. These budgets are prepared separately from operating budgets. Various techniques are adopted to evaluate the profitability of the project.

4.5 Areas of Financial Planning

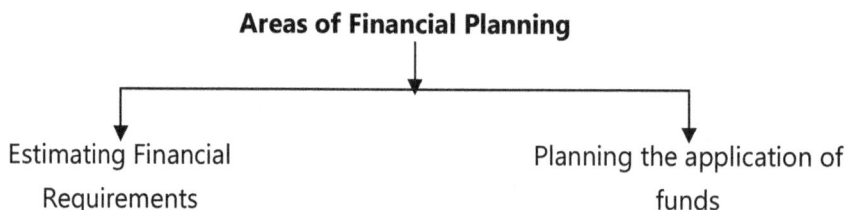

Areas of Financial Planning

Estimating Financial Requirements   Planning the application of funds

I. **Plans for estimating the financial requirements of the firm can be as follows:**

(i) **Planning Total Capitalisation:** This plan is prepared to estimate the total financial resources required by an organisation to attain the specified objectives. Poor planning may lead to overcapitalisation or undercapitalisation which has an adverse effect on cost leading to a decrease in the percentage profit. On the other hand, undercapitalisation, caused due to inaccurate planning, can lead to an increase in the profit percentage.

(ii) **Profit Planning:** Profit planning requires the preparation of various budgets such as sales budget, production budget, operating cost budget, purchase budget etc. Sales forecasting is the starting point. All the budgets are based on a sales forecast.

(iii) **Capital Structure Planning:** Capital structure refers to the debt equity mix in the capital structure of the company. The use of fixed cost bearing funds has to be done cautiously, as on one hand, it increases the EPS and on the other hand, affects the solvency of the company as interest on borrowings and debt repayment has to be made irrespective of whether the company is making profit or not. This balance between return and risk is called risk-return trade-off.

(iv) **Dividend Planning:** A company has to determine its dividend policy, in the sense, what percentage of profit it would retain and the percentage of profit, the company would distribute as dividend. Non-payment of dividend leads to conservation of cash reserves and profit for internal financing. On the other hand, it may affect the market sentiments. Internal financing, doesn't involve any cost in terms of payment of returns to the providers of funds. But, if dividend is not paid, some of the shareholders may not approve of it. A company has to balance these tax conflicting aspects of business i.e., liquidity and growth.

II. Plans for the application of funds:

Funds are applied to acquire fixed assets and for working capital needs of the organisation.

(i)   Fixed asset planning is also called capital budgeting. These decisions are crucial because these involve huge capital, the decisions are irreversible and they determine the future profitability of the business.

(ii)   Working capital requirement has to be planned. It is required to carry out the day-to-day activities of the organisation. Working capital determines the liquidity of the business. Working capital requirement and proper sources of financing of the working capital have to be decided.

4.6 Steps in Financial Planning

The following steps are involved in financial planning:

1.   Analysis of the firm's **past performance** to ascertain the relationships between financial variables, and the firm's financial strengths and weaknesses. A company can make use of such tools as ratio analysis, cash flow statement, trend analysis, common size and comparative financial statement etc.

2.   Analysis of firm's **operating characteristics:** product, market, competition, production and marketing policies, control system, operating risk etc., to decide its growth objective.

3.   Determining the firm's **investment needs** and choices, given its growth objectives and overall strategy.

4.   Forecasting the firm's **revenues and expenses** and need for funds based on its investment and dividend policies.

5.   Analysing **financial alternatives** within its financial policy and deciding the appropriate means of raising funds.

6.   Analysing the **consequences** of its financial plans for the long-term health and survival of the firm.

7.   Evaluating the **consistency of financial policies** with each other and with the corporate strategy.

4.7 Methods of Forecasting

There are a number of methods of business forecasting. These can be grouped into:

(i)   Qualitative techniques; and

(ii) Quantitative techniques.

Qualitative techniques are also called as subjective method, as these are based on the opinion of the end user or sales personnel. It is not based on data.

(a) Market research is one of the qualitative techniques. Under this method a survey is conducted to know the opinion of the prospective buyers. A large number of people are asked as to whether they would buy the product or service concerned when launched by the company. The advantage with this method is that the prospective customers are asked directly, hence the poll results are more likely to be accurate.

(b) Delphi method provides an alternative to market research. If the product is new, the field experts the sales persons who have knowledge about the customer's likes and dislikes, can be polled. Their opinion can be compiled as forecast.

Merits

(i)   This method is simple and does not involve the use of statistical techniques.

(ii)   The forecasts are based on firsthand knowledge of salesmen and others directly connected with sales.

(iii) This method may prove useful in forecasting the sales of new products.

Demerits

(i)   This method is almost subjective as personal opinions can possibly influence the forecast.

(ii)   The usefulness of this method is restricted to short term forecasting– for a period of less than one year.

(iii) The salesmen may be unaware of the impact of the broader economic changes (i.e. the secular changes) on future demand.

Quantitative techniques also known as objective method, removes the subjectivity of the people in the forecast. These methods use data rather than opinion to forecast.

(a) Regression and Correlation Analysis

This uses statistical and econometric techniques to investigate the nature and extent of relationship between variables. One of the variables may be time. A time series is a series of values of a dependent variable e.g. sales, as it changes from one point of time to another. Regression and correlation analysis explore the relation between a dependent variable, e.g. sales and independent variables, e.g. income, price, advertising expenditure etc. Such relationships, established from past data, may be used as a basis for predicting the future.

(b) Indicators

This approach of demand forecasting is based on certain economic indicators such as GDP, National income, rate of unemployment etc. Under this method relationship of these economic barometers and sales of a product or service is studied and established, with the help of certain statistical tools such as regression and correlation analysis, trend analysis, etc. On the basis of these statistical relationships, future demand and sales is predicted.

Merits

(i) These economic indicators are published by specialised organisations like the Central Stastical Organisation (CSO). This organisation publishes National Income estimates in India, hence they are reliable.

(ii) It removes subjectivity of people as it uses statistical tools and data.

Demerits

(i) Finding an appropriate economic indicator may be difficult.

(ii) This method is inappropriate for new products because no past data exists.

(c) Trend Projection

A firm which has been in existence for some time would have accumulated considerable data on sales pertaining to different time periods. Such data when arranged chronologically, yield time series. This data can be used to analyse the trend of sales of the product in question and can be extended to forecast the future demand.

Merit

This method is popular because it is simple and inexpensive.

Demerit

Trend in the past may not continue in future. Hence prediction based on past may not be correct.

Both the methods have their own merits and limitations. Qualitative methods are suitable for short term forecasting whereas the quantitative ones are meant for long term forecasting.

4.7.1 Financial Forecasting

Financial forecasting is the basis for financial planning. Forecasts are merely estimates based on past data. *"Financial forecasting refers to the formal process of predicting future events which are going to affect the functioning of the firm".* It helps to determine, in advance the requirement and utilisation of funds for a future period. It involves use of forecasting techniques. Some of the important forecasting techniques are:

1. **Percentage of Sales Method:** This is the simplest forecasting technique. Sales determine the financial needs of a firm. As per this technique, the different times of assets and liabilities, revenues are expressed as a percentage of sales. The required financial data is then developed for sales at different levels. For example, how much investment is required in Plant and Machinery if company wants to have sales of ₹ 10 crores.

2. **Simple Regression Method:** On the basis of the cause and effect relationship between sales and different items of cost, a regression line or line of best fit, can be drawn. On the basis of the regression line, the expenses and other items like debtors can be found out.

3. **Multiple Regression Analysis:** Under this technique the impact of other items on sales are also considered. In other words, sales is considered to be a function of other items.

4.8 Significance of Financial Planning

A sound financial plan provides the following benefits:

1. It helps to know potential financial problems before they actually occur. The plan sets the course of action to be taken to deal with crisis situations. Thus, the firm is not forced to take emergency financial decision without giving due weightage to all the important factors.

2. It provides a standard for financial performance which helps in comparing the actual performance with that of the standard set in the plans.

3. It helps in identifying the factors that determine the success and well being of the business.

4. Financial planning permits the management to focus on important, non-routine and critical matters, thereby saving the time and energy of the management.

5. Planning helps to optimize the use of the firm's financial resources through most profitable channels since it provides sufficient time to have the cost-benefit analysis of every course of action.

6. Planning co-ordinates, integrates and balances the efforts of the various departments, so as to achieve the overall objectives of an enterprise.

7. It provides sufficient time to fulfill the needed formalities to procure funds from the appropriate source of finance.

8. Financial planning includes the timing of procurement of the funds. This helps in maintaining solvency of the firm.

4.9 Limitations of Financial Planning

1. Financial forecasting is an integral part of financial planning. Forecasting uses past data to estimate the future financial requirements. Forecasting requires a good vision, judgement and experience. But the best knowledge may fail to forecast the future developments.

2. Financial planning is not a science. Its accuracy may suffer due the subjectivity of the management and their personal biases. Management may have vested interest which may be in conflict with the interests of the shareholders.

3. Financial forecasting in itself is not enough for the success of a financial plan. Effective implementation of the plan is of utmost importance.

4. There is a plan, doesn't mean that the management would just allow things to happen as per the plan. Continuous evaluation of plans must be done to get the best out of the set plans. If needed plans may be modified.

Points to Remember

- **Financial planning** pertains to the function of finance and includes the determination of the firm's financial objectives, formulating and promulgating financial policies and developing financial procedures.

- **Principles of a good financial plan:**
  (i) Simplicity
  (ii) Flexibility
  (iii) Liquidity
  (iv) Optimum use
  (v) Cost
  (vi) Co-ordination of long-term and short term financial plans

- **Types of Financial plans:**
  - (i)   Short term
  - (ii) Long term
- **Budget** is a financial or quantitative statement, prepared prior to a specified accounting period, containing the plans and policies to be pursued during the budget period.
- **Types of budgets:**
  - (i)   Operating budgets
  - (ii) Financial budgets
  - (iii) Capital budgets
- **Areas of financial planning:**
  - (i)   Estimating financial requirements
  - (ii) Planning the application of funds
- **Methods of forecasting:**
  - (i)   Qualitative techniques
  - (ii) Quantitative techniques

Questions for Discussion

1. Explain the concept of Financial Planning.
2. What are the objectives of Financial Planning?
3. Briefly enumerate the principles of a good financial plan.
4. Discuss the major areas of financial planning.
5. Write short notes on:
   - (a) Financial Forecasting
   - (b) Significance of Financial Planning
   - (c) Limitations of Financial Planning.
6. Explain the essentials of a good financial plan.
7. Write a short note on Budget.
8. Enumerate the steps involved in Financial planning. What is the significance of financial planning?
9. Explain the advantages and limitations of Financial planning.
10. What is Financial forecasting? Explain the methods of forecasting.
11. Give a brief account of the various types of plans.

Questions from Previous Pune University Examinations

1. Define Financial Planning. Also explain its advantages and limitations.   **[April 2009]**

2. Explain Process of Financial Planning in detail.   **[April 2009, Oct. 2009]**

3. Write short note on Limitations of Financial Planning.   **[April 2010]**

4. What is Financial Planning? Explain in detail objectives and process of 'Financial Planning'.   **[April 2010]**

5. Write short note Significance of Financial Planning.   **[Oct. 2010]**

6. What do you mean by Financial Planning? Explain in detail different objectives of Financial Planning.   **[April 2011]**

7. Write short note on Significance of Financial Planning.   **[Oct. 2011]**

8. What are the different steps involved in Financial Planning? What are the different characteristics of Financial Planning?   **[Oct. 2011]**

9. Write short note on Limitations of Financial Planning.   **[April 2012]**

10. Define Financial Planning. What is the significance of Financial Planning? Write in detail various steps involved in Financial Planning.   **[April 2012]**

11. What is Capitalisation? Explain in detail causes and consequences of Undercapitalisation.   **[April 2012]**

12. What do you mean by Financial Planning? What are the steps involved in Formulation of Financial Planning? Explain limitations of Financial Planning.   **[Oct. 2012]**

13. Write short note on steps involved in Financial Planning.   **[April 2013]**

14. Meaning of Financial Planning. What are the principles of Good Financial Planning? What are the limitations of Financial Planning.   **[April 2013]**

■■■

Chapter 5...

Recent Trends in Business Finance

Contents ...

Learning Objectives ...

➢ To understand the features of venture capital and venture capital investment process

➢ To comprehend leasing and types of leases

➢ To learn about microfinance

➢ To get acquainted with mutual funds, debt schemes, hybrid schemes and mutual fund schemes

Introduction

Business finance through equity shares, debentures, bonds, loans etc. are important conventional sources of finances. These are essential for all businesses. But all these sources may not be suitable at all times or to all people. For example, a firm in need for funds for asset financing may like to try an asset before actually buying it, or may like to use the available funds for working capital financing rather than using it as sunk capital. In such a situation lease financing may be a better option than borrowing. Further investors may not have the expertise to select the best investment option or may not be able to decide the portfolio of investment (proportion of funds to be invested in different avenues of investment). Mutual fund investment provides the needed expertise.

Some of the recent developments in the field of finance are discussed below.

5.1 Venture Capital

Venture capital is provided to entrepreneurs who want to start a high-tech untried project having risk and at the same time high potential of profits. It is also meant for those who have do not have long history of running businesses. Entrepreneurs who have new ideas of promising business but don't have funds, or cannot borrow due to the risk involved in the project, or due to hesitation of banks to finance such ideas, may approach venture capital institutions for finance. Venture capitalist, if they find the proposed business to be worthy, may provide equity i.e. invest in the proposal. They take part in the management of the business, provide guidance to the promoters and exit after 5 to 7 years by way of 'Initial Public Issue' (IPO). Thus they realise their investment and make capital gain if the company succeeds in the venture.

5.1.1 Definitions

1. According to Investopedia, *"money provided by investors to startup firms and small businesses with perceived long-term growth potential. This is a very important source of funding for start ups that do not have access to capital markets. It typically entails high risk for the investor, but it has the potential for above-average returns"*.

2. According to Oxford Dictionary of Business and Management *"Capital invested in a project in which there is a substantial element of risk, especially money invested in a new venture or an expanding business. Risk capital is normally invested in the equity of the company in the hope of high returns, it is not a loan."*

3. According to Webster's New World Finance and Investment Dictionary, "Money that is given to entrepreneurs to invest in a start-up business or to develop a product. Venture capital is very risky investment and those investing money may lose their entire investment. However, if the business or the product becomes successful, the return can be huge. Venture capital is raised by venture capital firms who solicit investment from institutional investors, such as banks, private equity units, pension funds, or other investment management firms, as well as from wealthy individuals. Venture capital investments are made at different stages, with some venture capitalists focusing only on seed or initial investments, others on middle stages firms and others on later stage companies that have a viable product that is producing revenue."

4. The 1995 Finance Bill, defines Venture Capital as *"long-term equity investment in novel technology, based projects with display potential for significant growth and financial returns"*.

New business ideas or untried ideas are very risky. The ideas may turn out to be a success and generate huge profits or may fail in which case the capitalist would lose everything invested. Firm of investors or wealthy individuals may be interested in taking the risk of providing funds for such business ideas in the form of equity and may exit after few years when their capital appreciates.

5.1.2 Characteristic Features of Venture Capital

1. Capital investment may be in the form of either equity or debt or both as a derivative Instrument.
2. It is made in hi-tech projects involving high risk and strong potential of high profitability.
3. Venture capitalist finance the projects and wait for 5 to 7 years to reap the benefit of capital appreciation.
4. Venture capital funds is not repaid rather is realised through exit route.
5. The exit route may be any of the following:
   (i)   Public issue of shares,
   (ii) Sale of share to entrepreneurs,
   (iii) Sale of company to another company,
   (iv) Finding new investor, or
   (v)   Liquidation.
6. Venture capital organisation may be wholly owned subsidiaries of financial institutions, or owned by Government, or may be a group of individual venture capitalists.
7. The financing of high-tech projects in the form of venture capital is done in various stages.
8. Venture capitalists become member of the board in order to closely watch the performance of the business unit. The claim over management is decided on the basis of proportion of investment.

5.1.3 Venture Capital Investment Process

Financing of novel **high-tech** project under venture capital has following process:

1. **Contact between entrepreneur and venture capitalist:** The prospective entrepreneur prepares project report and makes a formal application to venture capital investor. This can be done with the help of auditor, banker or professionals. It consists of five important feasibility report – technical, financial, managerial, marketing, and socio-economic feasibility.

2. **Preliminary evaluation:** after receiving the application the venture capitalist goes through the project report and if they find the deal worthwhile they may establish contact with the management to make a detailed appraisal of the project. The management team of the venture is required to present the detailed model of the company, unique aspects of the proposed business, future prospects and investment proposal. During the interaction with the management team the venture capitalist assess the quality and competence of the management team. If the venture capitalist finds the proposal investible proposition, a document containing terms of proposed investment is devised and negotiated with promoter. This is called term sheet.

3. **Detailed analysis:** after getting the approval of the promoters on the terms of proposed investment, the detailed analysis of the project is carried out. During this stage of the business, financial and legal aspects of the project is examined. The risk is assessed through **sensitivity analysis**. The requirement of funds, stages and quantum of investment is also assessed. On successful completion of the analysis, the venture capitalist may modify or stipulate other conditions that are considered by them for investment in the company, and negotiate changes in the term sheet with the entrepreneurs. In case the revised terms are agreeable to the entrepreneurs, venture capitalist issues '**Letter of Intent**' for investment in the venture and require the investee company to complete formalities for availing the investment. These formalities include execution of the legal agreement by promoter, passing of requisite Board resolution, obtaining approval of the govt., and other statutory approvals for investment.

4. **Investment:** on getting a formal request from the company for release of investment the venture capitalist make investment in the company as per the agreement.

5. **Monitoring the project:** the progress of the project shall be monitored by the venture capitalist. An executive director is appointed for the purpose by the venture capitalist. The venture capitalist give inputs on strategic plans and guide the company for optimising its performance.

5.1.4 Exit Route of Venture Capitalist

The aim of venture capitalist is to realise huge profit on exiting the venture after some period of functioning of the venture. The venture capitalist may exit the company by adopting any of the following modes:

(a) **Going public:** Most of the venture capital firms prefer to go in for public issue to recover their investment with profits. The company makes public issue of its shares. The shares are listed on stock exchange. By selling the shares at premiums the venture capital firms make profit on their investment and exit the company.

(b) Sale of shares to entrepreneurs/companies: Instead of selling shares in the primary market, it is sold to entrepreneurs or to other companies, who may be interested in taking over the venture due to its high profit potential.

(c) Liquidation: If the project performs badly, it may be closed down.

Venture capital in India: history of venture capital in India dates back to the early 70s when Government of India appointed a committee headed by R.S.Bhatt to find out new methods of funding start-up companies that are ready to bring innovative technologies. The committee recommended starting of venture capital Industry in India. In 80s financial institutions like ICICI, IDBI, IFCI came forward to fund small technological companies.

Venture capital institutions are regulated by guidelines issued by the 'Controller of Capital Issues" (CCI) in India. The World Bank chose 6 institutions to start venture capitalist investment in India. These included – TDICICI (ICICI), GVFL, Canbank venture capital Fund, APIDC, RCTC (now known as IFCI venture capital Fund Ltd.) and ILF.

In 1995 Govt. of India permitted Foreign finance companies to make investment in India. Many foreign venture capitalist Firms entered India. Government has been issuing guidelines to regulate the venture capitalist industry.

5.2 Leasing

Lease is one of the methods of financing the fixed assets of an enterprise. An enterprise with inadequate funds for financing the investment in plant and machinery may enter into lease agreement with the owners of the assets. The contract of lease allows the lessee to use the asset for a certain period in return for a periodical payment. After the expiry of the period the lease agreement may renewed or the asset may be purchased by the lessee if so desired by the lessee.

5.2.1 Definitions

1. **Herbert B. Mayo:** *"a contract for the use of an asset such as plant or equipment. The firm that owns the asset permits the lessee to use the goods. In return the lessor enters into a contract (the lease) to make specific payments for the use of the asset. The lease is usually for a specified time period and may be renewable."*

2. **Merriam Webster dictionary:** *"a legal agreement that lets someone use a car, house etc., for a period of time in return for payment. It is a contract by which one conveys real estate, equipment, or facilities for a specified term and for a specified rent."*

3. **Raymond G. Schultz:** *"the user agrees to pay a rental charge and adhere to other conditions of a lease contract in return for the right to utilise property of the owner in his operations for a specified period."*

5.2.2 Characteristic Features of Leasing

1. It is a contract between lessor and lessee.
2. The contract gives a right to the lessee to use an asset in return for a payment.
3. The contract is for a limited period of time but can be renewed for a further period.
4. Lessor is the owner of the asset.
5. On the expiry of the period of lease, the lessor may sell the asset to the lessee or the any other party.

5.2.3 Types of Lease

Leases are classified into different types based on the variations in the elements of the lease agreement. Most popular classification of lease is financial lease and operating lease. Apart from these, there are sale and lease back and direct lease, single investor lease and leveraged lease, and domestic and international lease. The variations can be in certain elements of the lease agreement as follows:

(i)   The degree of ownership risk and rewards transferred to the lessee;
(ii) Location of the lessor, lessee and the equipment supplier;
(iii) Number of parties involved;

I. Financial Lease and Operating Lease

Financial lease is also called as Full Pay-out lease. Under this kind of lease agreement, the lessor transfers substantially all the risks and rewards associated with the asset to the lessee. The ownership gets transferred at the end of the economic life of the asset. Lease term is spread over the major part of the asset's life. It has the following features:

- It is for a long period of time, normally equal to the expected useful life of the asset;
- It is not cancellable;
- Usually the maintenance of the property, property taxes and insurance is provided by the lessee;
- The risk and rewards associated with the lease is transferred to the lessee;
- The burden of obsolescence falls on the lessee.

The companies that frequently update or replace equipment and want to use equipment for less than its economic life may not like to go for financial lease. Operating lease does not run for full economic life of the asset, and the lessee is not liable for financing its full value. Lessor carries the risk associated with the asset. Maintenance, property taxes and insurance are usually provided by the lessor. Thus along with the right to use the property, the lessee obtains some services also. The main features of operating lease are:

- Normally leasing of the assets is the regular business of the lessor;
- In most of the cases, the lease is cancellable at the instance of the lessor;
- The lease period id relatively short, not exceeding 2 or 3 years;

- The capital cost of the asset cannot be recovered from one such lease of the asset as the lease period is short. Hence the lessor leases the property a number of times either to the same lessee or to another lessee;
- The maintenance of the property, the payment of property taxes and insurance usually falls on the lessor.
- The risk of obsolescence falls on the lesssor.

II. Sale and Lease Back

Under this method of lease the owner of an asset sells the asset to another person without giving away the possession of the asset. The purchaser of the asset now becomes owner of the property and enters into a lease agreement with the vendor of the asset who becomes the lessee after the contract of lease. The original owner pays rentals for use of the asset to the current owner of the asset. Thus under sale and lease back seller becomes the lessee and the buyer becomes the lessor of the property.

III. Leveraged Lease

Under leveraged leasing arrangement, the lessor borrows funds to buy the asset meant to be leased out. Around 80% of the cost of the asset is borrowed from a third party on the security of the asset. The asset is leased out in the regular manner. The lease rental received from the lessee is used to repay the loan.

IV. Direct Leasing

Under direct leasing, a firm acquires the right to use an asset from the manufacturer directly. The ownership o the asset remains with the manufacturer.

V. Big Ticket Leasing

This method of leasing is more popular for very expensive assets such as construction equipment, sophisticated computer system, heavy machinery etc. The cost of asset is so huge that it may not be possible for one lessor to provide the asset on lease. Two or more lessor companies join hands in leasing. The asset may be funded by the lessors themselves or they might finance partly by the lessors and partly lender of it and the rest may be financed by borrowed funds.

VI. Cross Broader Leasing

When the lessor and the lessee belong to different countries the leasing arrangement is called as cross broader leasing.

VII. Inhouse Leasing

When a group of companies promote a leasing company for the benefit of the companies in the group, the company is called the 'inhouse leasing company'. Inhouse leasing company provides a lot of benefits to the group companies.

VIII. On the basis of the Terms of Payment

  (i)   **Balloon rental leasing:** here the initial rent amounts are lower and the rent amount increases during the later period of the lease.

  (ii)   **Step rental leasing:** under this arrangement the rent amount is not fixed for the whole of the period of lease. It depends upon the size of income flow of the lessee.

  (iii)   **Front heavy type leasing:** according to this arrangement, larger rentals are collected in the initial period of the lease and lower amount of rent is charged during the later part of the lease.

  (iv)   **Skipped payment leasing:** under this arrangement, rentals of certain periods, when the equipment is not functioning, is skipped.

  (v)   **Trial period leasing:** under this arrangement the lessee is allowed to take lease on a trial basis for sometime before deciding to take the asset on lease.

Advantages of Leasing

  (i)   Lessee gets the benefit of use of the asset without making any payment towards the purchase of the asset. Funds thus saved can be used for working capital requirements.

  (ii)   The lease agreement can be made to suit the needs of the lessee and lessor. There is lot of flexibility.

  (iii)   It is a cheaper source of financing when compared to debt financing.

  (iv)   The rent paid is chargeable to the profit and loss account of the lessee. Thus the lessee gets tax advantage.

Disadvantages of Leasing

  (i)   The lessor usually charges higher rate of interest than the rate he pays on borrowings.

  (ii)   The residual value of the asset may accrue to the lessor.

5.3 Microfinance

Banking facilities like loan, overdraft, saving money etc. may not be accessible to low income groups of the society and people living below poverty line. Microfinance is a form of financial services for entrepreneurs and small business lacking access to banking related services.

Definitions

Investopedia: "a type of banking service that is provided to unemployed or low-income individuals or groups who would otherwise have no other means of gaining financial services. Ultimately, the goal of microfinance is to give low income people an opportunity to become self-sufficient by providing a means of saving money, borrowing money and insurance".

The essential features of microfinance are:

- Loans are given without security.
- It is meant for those living below poverty line, and members of self-help groups(SHG), such as street vendors, small artisans, small household entrepreneurs. The selection of client is made by NGOs.
- Maximum limit of loan under microfinance is ₹ 25,000.
- The terms and conditions of loans and the people to whom loan is given is decided by the NGOs (Non- government organisations).
- Often fresh loans are granted if the previous loan is repaid. Thus this is a permanent arrangement.
- The interest charged is higher as the clients do not have salary, and also because no security is asked be MFIs for loans.

Difference between microcredit and microfinance

Microfinance is a wider concept when compared to micro credit since besides loan many other services such as insurance, health services, saving etc are provided to the borrower. Micro credit typically refers to very small loans given to unsalaried borrowers with little or no collateral.

Microfinance Institutions: the micro finance institutions normally start as not-for-profit organisations like NGOs, Credit unions and other financial co-operatives and state owned development banks. Financial institutions may come up exclusively to give micro finance facilities. Commercial banks may have a microfinance department.

Microfinance in India:

NABARD started microfinance in India. As per the concept developed by it, the SHG, NGO and Banks are to be linked. Self help groups are formed and nurtured by the NGOs. These groups learn thrift, and banking operations. On accomplishing a certain degree of maturity in monetary activities, the members of the self help groups are allowed to seek credit from the bank. NGO play major role in linking the groups with the banks.

5.4 Mutual Fund

Investors like to maximise their returns and minimise their risk. Diversified portfolio can help achieve this objective. But all investors may not have the time or the expertise to take decisions regarding diversification of investment. Mutual fund investment caters to the needs of such investors. By participating in a scheme of mutual fund, the investor becomes a part owner of all the investments held under the scheme, in the same proportion as the scheme. Every unit will have the same proportion of debt and equity as is the scheme.

Mutual funds are investment companies that invest the funds collected from the sale of their units or shares, in different classes of assets, on behalf of their unit holders or share holders. Mutual fund is a portfolio of investment. Small investors who don't possess knowledge and who are not ready to take risk may depend on mutual funds. Investors can buy the units of mutual fund and become its member. The fund managers would manage the funds of the members and make investment on behalf of the investors and distribute the profits from the investments to its members.

5.4.1 Types of Mutual Funds

(A) Mutual funds schemes on the basis of Asset Mix

Mutual fund schemes can be classified on the basis of asset-mix into three broad categories:

(i) Equity schemes
(ii) Debt schemes; and
(iii) Hybrid schemes

(i) Equity Schemes

These schemes invest around 85% to 95% of the funds in equity shares or equity linked instruments and the balance in cash. Equity schemes can be:

(a) **Diversified Equity Scheme:** Under this scheme wide range of industries are chosen for investment. It invests in the equity of diversed industries. For example the portfolio may consist of investment in FMCG, Petroleum and oil, agro based industries, pharmaceutical, automotive industries, banks etc.

(b) **Index Schemes:** This scheme invests in the equities that are listed in a stock exchange. For example if 30 stocks are listed in sensex, then in those 30 stocks investment will be made by the mutual fund in the same proportion as the respective equity base of the 30 companies. The index scheme appreciates or depreciates in the same way as the concerned index.

(c) **Sectoral Schemes:** These schemes invest in the equity stocks of a given sector, for example: steel sector, banking sector, power sector etc.

(d) **Tax Planning Schemes:** These schemes invest in such equity stocks that reduce the tax liability of the investor. For example the unit linked schemes of Reliance Tax saver (ELSS).

(e) **Arbitrage schemes:** These schemes purchase securities in the spot market and sell them in the future markets. There is a difference in the price of spot market and future markets. Spot market prices are typically lower than the prices in the futures market. On or before the expiry date of the futures contract, the difference between the two market prices disappears. At that time the position is unwound to book the profit.

(ii) Debt Schemes

As the name suggest these schemes invest in the debt instruments viz; bonds and cash. Debt schemes may assume any of the following schemes:

(a) **Gilt Schemes:** Under the scheme investment is made only in the government bonds and 10 to 15 percent of pooled funds in cash. Examples are UTI G-sec., Tata GSF

(b) **Mixed Debt Schemes:** These schemes invest in government bonds, corporate bonds and cash. 30 to 40 percent of funds are invested in govt. Bonds , 40 to 55 percent in corporate bonds and balance is invested in cash. For example UTI bond.

(c) **Floating Rate Debt Schemes:** These funds invest in a portfolio comprising substantially of floating rate debt and bonds. For example Grindlays Floating rate schemes.

(d) **Cash Schemes:** These schemes are also called as liquid schemes. These schemes invest in the money markets instruments like Treasury Bills, commercial paper, certificate of deposits, call money, reverse repos and deposits with banks. They also have around 25% of their fund investment in short-term bonds.

(e) **Fixed Maturity Plan:** It is an important debt scheme. It is a closed ended scheme that has a fixed maturity. The maturity period ranges between three months to three years. The funds of the scheme are invested primarily in corporate bonds.

(iii) Hybrid Schemes

These schemes invest in both equity and debt instruments. A hybrid scheme may be equity oriented or debt oriented or has a variable ratio of the two instruments. A hybrid scheme where the proportion of equity investment is more is called the equity oriented scheme and where debt proportion is more is termed as debt-oriented scheme.

A hybrid scheme may vary the proportion of debt and equity based on the market conditions. The equity proportion in such schemes increase when the market falls and decrease when market price rise. It is good to buy/invest in equity when the price is low and is better to sell when the market price is high.

(B) Mutual fund Schemes on the basis of Trading Possibility

On the basis of trading possibility , mutual fund can be classified into:

(i) Open-ended schemes

(ii) Closed-ended schemes

(i) **Open-ended schemes:** These schemes allow the investors to subscribe and sell the units of the fund on a continuous basis. There is no fixed maturity period for the units. These schemes are not listed in a secondary market. The Net Asset Value(NAV) is declared on a daily basis. The investors can purchase units on a continuous basis and sell or withdraw their funds under a re-purchase arrangement. The subscribers to the scheme get a value closer to the NAV.

(ii) **Closed ended schemes:** These schemes are open for the investors only for a limited period of time, usually one month to three months. The investors can not withdraw their investment as and when they want. These schemes have a maturity period ranging between 5 to 15 years. These schemes are listed on stock exchange. Investors can withdraw from the scheme by selling their units in the secondary market. The price quoted on the stock exchange is much less than the NAV of the units.

Difference between Open-ended and Closed-ended Schemes

(i) **Period:** The subscription to a closed ended scheme is kept open only for a limited period, usually one month to three months. The subscription to an open-ended scheme is allowed on a continuous basis.

(ii) **Withdrawal of funds:** A closed ended scheme does not allow its investors to withdraw funds as and when they like. An open-ended scheme on the other hand allows the investors to withdraw funds under re-purchase arrangement.

(iii) **Maturity period:** A closed ended scheme has a specific maturity period say 5 to 15 years. An open-ended scheme does not have a maturity period.

(iv) **Listing on stock exchange:** The units of closed-ended scheme are listed on stock exchange. The open-ended schemes are not listed on stock exchanges.

(v) **Net asset value (NAV):** In the secondary market the shares of closed-ended schemes sell at a discount (5% to 20%) over their NAV. On the other hand the subscriber to a closed ended scheme gets a value close to (0 to 2 percent) NAV on withdrawal.

(vi) **Performance:** The fund managers of closed-ended scheme can perform better as the funds are available for use for the entire period of the scheme.

The performance of an open-ended scheme gets adversely affected due to sharp inflow and outflow of funds i.e., changing amount of funds may cause difficulty in its management.

Advantages and Disadvantages of Mutual Funds

Advantages:

(i) **Diversification:** Mutual funds usually spread their investment across various industries and asset classes like banking companies, food industries, land, gold, government bonds etc. Diversification reduces risk. An investor of mutual fund thus gets the benefits of diversification.

(ii) **Professional management:** Mutual funds are managed by professionals who are experienced in the field. They have education, skill and resources to know about the investment opportunities. Mutual fund investors get benefit of their expertise.

(iii) **Liquidity:** An open-ended scheme, allows the unit holders to redeem their units by paying a fee called exit-load. On the other hand closed-ended schemes are listed on the stock exchange, that allows the investors to sell off their units in the stock markets whenever they want to withdraw their funds. Thus both the schemes provide liquidity to the investment.

(iv) **Return potential:** Equity oriented schemes have potential for higher returns.

(v) **Tax benefits:** Dividend received from equity-oriented mutual funds is tax free. Besides investment in certain mutual funds is deductible from the total income of individual assesses.

(vi) **Regulations:** Mutual funds in India are regulated and monitored by the Securities and Exchange Board of India (SEBI). The interest of the investors is well protected.

Disadvantages:

(i) **Dependence on manager's skill:** the investor in mutual funds places his money in the hands of the managers of the fund. The return on the investment depends on the skill and judgments of the manager.

(ii) **Cost:** mutual funds charge fees for management and various administrative services. The fees can reduce the return on investment.

(iii) **Redemption of mutual funds:** although redemption of mutual funds is allowed but the return could get adversely affected due to sales commission and redemption fees.

Points to Remember

- **Venture capital** is financial capital provided to early-stage, high-potential, high risk, growth startup companies.

- Money provided by investors to startup firms and small businesses with perceived long-term growth potential. This is a very important source of funding for startups that do not have access to capital markets. It typically entails high risk for the investor, but it has the potential for above-average returns.

- **Venture Capital Investment Process:**
    (i)   Contact between entrepreneur and venture capitalist
    (ii) Preliminary evaluation
    (iii) Detailed analysis
    (iv) Investment
    (v)   Monitoring the project

- **Exit Route of Venture Capitalist:**
    - (i)   Going public
    - (ii) Sale of shares to entrepreneurs / companies
    - (iii) Liquidation
- **Leasing** is a process by which a firm can obtain the use of a certain fixed assets for which it must pay a series of contractual, periodic, tax deductible payments.
- The lessee is the receiver of the services or the assets under the lease contract and the lessor is the owner of the assets.
- **Types of Lease:**
    - (i)   Financial lease and operating lease
    - (ii)   Sale and lease back
    - (iii) Leveraged lease
    - (iv)   Direct leasing
    - (v)   Big ticket leasing
    - (vi)   Cross broader leasing
    - (vii) In house leasing
    - (viii) On the basis of the terms of payment
- **Microfinance** is a form of financial services for entrepreneurs and small businesses lacking access to banking and related services.
- The two main mechanisms for the delivery of financial services to such clients are:
    1. relationship-based banking for individual entrepreneurs and small businesses; and
    2. group-based models, where several entrepreneurs come together to apply for loans and other services as a group.
- **Mutual Fund**: A mutual fund is a type of professionally managed collective investment vehicle that pools money from many investors to purchase securities. While there is no legal definition of the term "mutual fund", it is most commonly applied only to those collective investment vehicles that are regulated and sold to the general public. They are sometimes referred to as "investment companies" or "registered investment companies."
- **Types of Mutual funds:**
    - (i)   Equity schemes
    - (ii) Debt schemes
    - (iii) Hybrid scheme

Questions for Discussion

I. **Choose the appropriate answer:**

1. Finance provided to street vendors is an example of:
   (a) Venture capital
   (c) Micro credit
   (b) Personal loans
   (d) Micro finance

2. Lessor, lessee and lendor are parties to:
   (a) Financial lease
   (c) Operating lease
   (b) Leveraged lease
   (d) Sell and lease back

3. NAV stands for:
   (a) Net asset value
   (b) Nominal asset value
   (c) Normal assigned value
   (d) Nominal assigned value.

4. NAV of mutual fund unit is announced for the:
   (a) Closed-ended fund
   (b) Open-ended fund
   (c) Hybrid fund
   (d) Equity fund

5. Mutual fund is:
   (a) An investment made in equity b.
   (b) Is a portfolio of investment
   (c) An investment made in bond
   (d) An institution providing consultancy services to the investors.

6. Venture capitalist exit through:
   (a) Public issue
   (c) Sale of shares to entrepreneurs
   (b) Finding new investor
   (d) Any of the three methods.

II. **Questions:**

1. Define the term venture capital. State its characteristic features.
2. Explain the process of venture capital investment.
3. Write a note on venture capital in India.

4. How would you differentiate venture capital with that of equity share capital?

5. What is leasing? Explain the different types of leasing.

6. What are the advantages and disadvantages associated with lease financing?

7. Differentiate 'operating lease' with that of 'financial lease'.

8. What is micro finance? State its essential features. How does microfinance work?

9. What is mutual fund? Discuss its types.

10. What are the advantages and disadvantages of mutual funds?

11. What are the differences between 'open-ended' and 'closed-ended' mutual fund?

III. Case study:

Hari Kisan is living with his family in a small village Handia in Kalahandi district of Orissa. He works in a farm as an agricultural worker. The income is not regular as he is a temporary employee. He gets work in the farm only in the sowing and harvesting seasons. He does not have funds to do any business. He is not educated enough to apply for jobs in the nearby towns.

Advice him as to what he can do to earn a decent regular income to sustain himself and his family.

■■■

Additional Important Concepts in Finance

(A) Agency Problem

In the corporate form of business, ownership and management is separated. The owners do not manage the affairs of the company. The following factors have contributed to the separation:

1. Companies need huge amount of funds to reduce their cost of production. These funds are obtained by issuing shares to a very large number of shareholders. It is not practically possible for all owners to participate in the management.

2. Companies need professional managers to run the business.

3. Separation of ownership and management facilitates change in the ownership through share transfers.

4. Investors like to maintain a diversified portfolio of securities. That is possible only when ownership and management are separated.

(B) Conflicting Interest

The problem with separation of ownership and management is the conflict in the interest of the owners and the managers. Managers enjoy the following:

1. Good remunerations and lavish perquisites.

2. Power of presiding over a big enterprise i.e. substantial autonomy in management.

Since, Directors enjoy autonomy and owners meet only once in a year, the managers/directors can pursue them personal goals. They may try to maintain an average level of performance in order to protect their job and may try to maximise their welfare. Thus, the welfare of the shareholders may take a back seat. Directors may participate in the management of the company and at the same time pursue their personal pet projects.

In order to reduce the agency problems, effective monitoring has to be done. As far as possible incentives may be based on performance. An attempt can be made to limit managerial discretion in certain areas. The performance of the manager may be reviewed periodically. Performance shares may be given. The purchase and sale of shares by the Directors must be monitored closely.

(C) Profit Plan

Profit plan is a short-term financial plan. It serves as a guide to the management in achieving the objectives of the firm. A profit plan is also called as a Budget. The features of a Budget are:

1. It is expressed in financial terms.

2. It is a future plan for a specified period.

3. It is a plan for the firms operators and resources.

4. It is a coordinated plan.

1. Financial Terms

Budgets are prepared in terms of units initially. But later, these are expressed in terms of money. For instance, sale budgets may state the number of units to be sold, production budget contains the units to be produced in the stated period, purchase budget show the units of materials to be purchased for meeting the budgeted production and labour budget shows the number of employees and labour hours. But, all these budgets can not be integrated in the absence of a common denominator. Cash is the common denominator. Hence, budgets are expressed in financial terms.

2. Specified Period

A budget is meaningful only when it is related to a specified period of time. The budget showing the number of labour hours required is irrelevant if the budget is not related to the period within which the stated number of labour hours are to be used.

3. Operations and Resources

A budget covers all the operations of a business firm. It matches the revenues and expenses for the operations. It contains plans regarding the resources necessary to carry out operations.

4. Integrated Plan

A budget for each operation is prepared and is integrated through a master budget. A firm may start with computing the sales forecast for the stated period. On the basis of the sales forecast, the sales budget is prepared, for the needed sales production is decided, to produce the needed output material requirements is determined and so on.

Budgets and forecasts, both refer to the anticipated actions and events in a specified future period. However, there are wide differences between the two:

Budget	Forecast
1. It refers to the policy and programme to be followed in a future period under planned conditions.	1. Forecast is concerned with probable events likely to happen under anticipated conditions during a specified period of time.
2. It is usually planned for each accounting period.	2. It may cover a long period of time.
3. It is integrated in the sense that sectional budgets are co-ordinated.	3. It may cover a specified function or activity, for e.g. sales budget.
4. Budgeting begins after the forecast.	4. The function of forecast ends with the forecast of likely events.

Performa of Sales Budget

| Sales Budget |

Year 2007-08

Area	Production	For the year			Per month	
		Quantity	Rate (₹)	Value (₹)	Quantity	Value (₹)
North	Product A					
	Product B					
	Product C					
South	Product A					
	Product B					
	Product C					
East	Product A					
	Product B					
	Product C					
West	Product A					
	Product B					
	Product C					
Total	Product A					
	Product B					
	Product C					

Proforma Production Budget

Year 2008

Department: Production

Months	Qty. of Sales	Add. Qty. of Closing Stock	Less Qty. of Opening Stock	Production Units to be completed	Add equivalent units in the closing w-in-p	Less equivalent units in the opening w-in-p	Total units
January							
February							
March							
April							
May							
June							
July							
August							
September							
October							
November							
December							
Total							

Cash Budget for the quarter ending 31st December, 2007

Particulars	October 2007	November 2007	December 2007
Opening Balance	5,000	5,680	(7,084)
Receipts:			
Sales collection	15,680	22,736	16,248
Credit sales collection			
20% of the same month	52,000	32,000	46,400
40% of the second month	48,000	52,000	32,000
Income from insurance claim			
(A)	**1,25,680**	**1,12,416**	**1,61,500**

Contd.

Payments:			
Purchases	1,00,000	1,04,000	1,06,000
Wages:			
75% of the same month	6,000	7,500	6,000
25% of the previous month	3,000	2,000	2,500
Miscellaneous Expenses	8,000	6,000	12,000
Rent	3,000	–	25,000
(B)	**1,20,000**	**1,19,500**	**1,51,500**
Closing Balance (A) – (B)	**5,680**	**(7,084)**	**10,000**

Proforma Manpower Budget

Manpower Budget

Classification of Labour	Grade I	Grade II	Grade III	Total	Present Strength	To be recruited
I. Direct Labour:						
Dept. X						
Dept. Y						
Dept. Z						
Sub. Total						
II. Indirect Labour:						
(a) Production						
(b) Administration						
(c) Selling and Distribution						
(d) Research and Development						
Sub Total						
(III) Total (I + II)						

Master Budget

Period

Normal Capacity	Budget Capacity							
	Product A		Product B		Product C		Total	
	Current Yr. (₹)	Previous Yr. (₹)	Current Yr. (₹)	Previous Yr. (₹)	Current Yr. (₹)	Previous Yr. (₹)	Current Yr. (₹)	Previous Yr. (₹)
Sales								
Less: Factory cost								
Gross Profit								
Less: Operating Expenses:								
Administration								
Selling & Distribution								
Research Development								
Opening Profit								
Add: Other Income								
Net profit before Tax								
Net Profit								
Less: Appropriations								
Profit Balance								
Assets:								
Fixed								
Current								
Total Capital employed								
Less: Outsiders liabilities:								
Current								
Long-term								
Shareholders Funds								

(D) Capital Structure Theories

Capital structure theories explain the theoretical relationship between cost of capital and the value of a firm. These important theories are:

1. Net Income (NI) approach
2. Net Operating Income (NOI) approach
3. Modigilani and Miller (MM) approach and
4. Traditional approach.

Net Income Approach

According to the Net Income approach, capital structure causes a change in the cost of capital and hence, the total value of the firm. As per the approach, as the usage of debt increases, a less costly source of capital is substituted for a more expensive one. It is possible for a firm to evolve a capital mix which minimises the cost of capital and maximises the value of the firm.

Net Operating Income (NOI) Approach

According to this approach, a change in the debt-equity ratio is irrelevant. A change in the leverage doesn't change the value of the firm. The justification is – as more and more debt is used, the financial risk (risk of insolvency) increases. To compensate for this increased risk shareholders would require a high rate of return on investment. Thus, the decrease in the cost of debt is offset by the increase in the cost of equity (i.e. expectations of the owners).

Modigilani and Miller (MM) Approach

This approach is similar to the NOI approach. The MM approach gives a behavioural justification for the constant cost of capital. According to this approach, cost and value of the firm is not affected by change in the debt-equity mix. According to MM, if two firms with the same EBIT have different values, the investors would sell their securities in the firm having higher market value and would invest in the company with lower market value, thereby increasing the number of shares held. The increased number of shares would earn a higher dividend. This process of switching will continue till the two firms with the same risk, show equal market value. This process is called the arbitrage process. Arbitrage process will have the following effects:

(i) lower the price of shares of the firm whose shares are sold;

(ii) increase the price of the firm where shares are being purchased.

Traditional Approach

This approach is mid-way between the NI and NOI approaches. According to this approach, a firm can increase its value and reduce the cost of capital by a judicious combination of debt and equity. However, beyond a certain point, the risk to the investors, as well as the creditors would increase. The increased cost would reduce the value of the firm. At that point the capital structure is optimum.

Net Income Approach

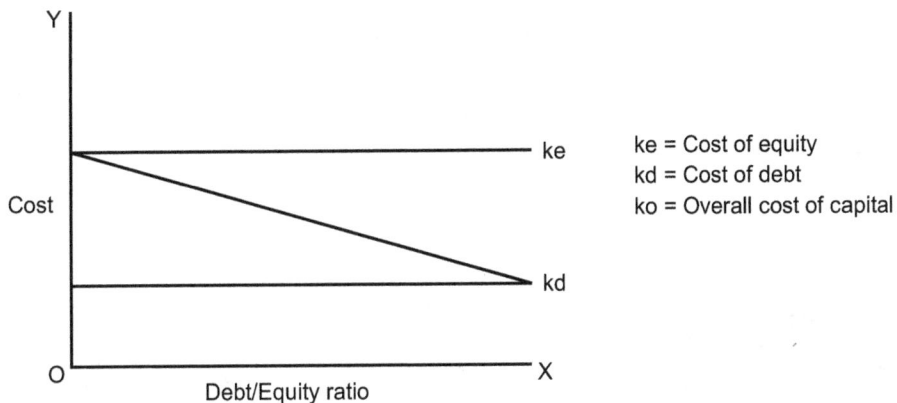

ke = Cost of equity
kd = Cost of debt
ko = Overall cost of capital

Fig.

Net Operating Income Approach

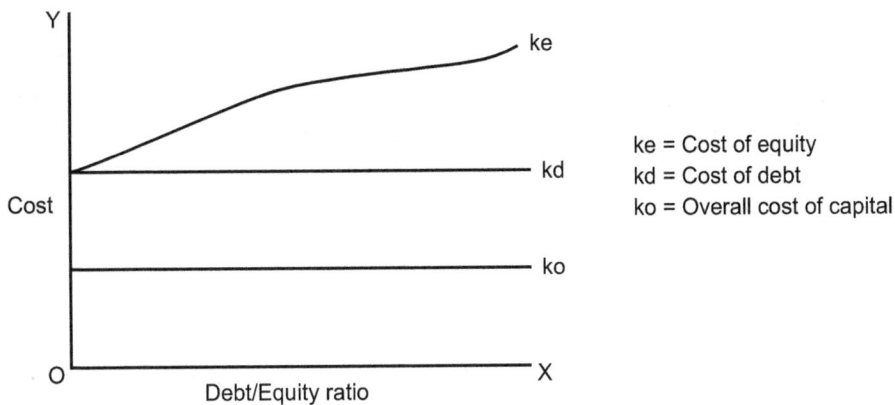

ke = Cost of equity
kd = Cost of debt
ko = Overall cost of capital

Fig.

MM Approach

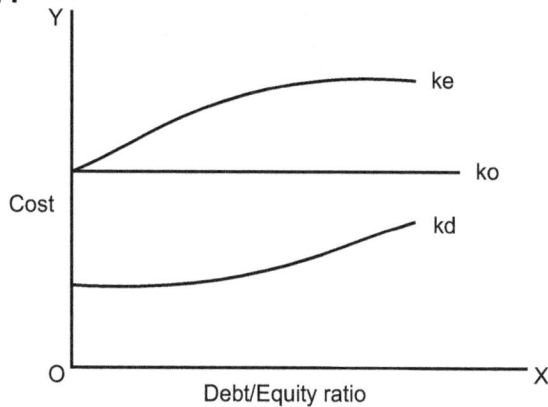

ke = Cost of equity
kd = Cost of debt
ko = Overall cost of capital

Fig.

Traditional Approach

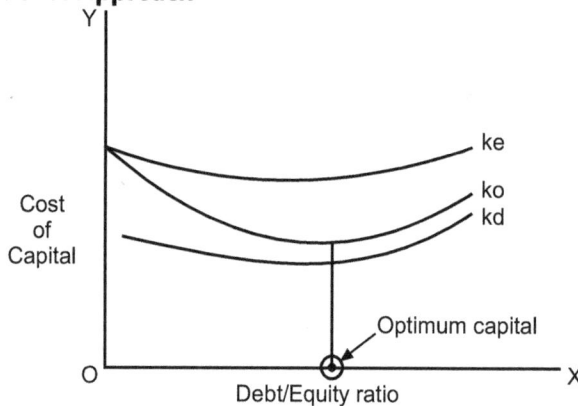

ke = Cost of equity
kd = Cost of debt
ko = Overall cost of capital

Fig.

(E) Risk

Risk is a possibility of financial loss (either in absolute terms or relative to expectations) that is inseparable from the opportunity for financial gain. Some of the major categories of risk are:

- Market risk
- Credit risk
- Liquidity risk; and
- Operational risk.

Material risk arises from changes in prices in financial markets. Credit risk relates to the failure of payment. Liquidity risk is that of running out of cash to meet day-to-day obligations. Operational risk is a catch-all category that covers a firm's internal systems and processes, as well as external events.

(I) Business Risk

Business risk is the risk that is inherent in the business operations of a company. It is caused by factors other than factors concerned with capital structure. Some of these factors are detailed below:

(a) Company related factors:

    (i)   Labour relation

    (ii) Managerial competence

    (iii) Competitive position

    (iv) Assets structures etc.

(b) Industry related factors:

    (i)   Growth prospects of the industry

    (ii) Trade unions

(c) Economic factors:

    (i)   Rate of inflation

    (ii) Recession

    (iii) Devaluation

    (iv) Government policy

Measurement of Business Risk

One of the widely used methods of measurement of business risk is by 'coefficient of variation' of the net operating income before for (EBIT). It is the ratio of standard deviation of expected value (mean).

$$\text{C.V.} = \frac{\sigma}{\overline{x}}$$

σ = Standard deviation of expected EBIT

$\overline{x}$ = Expected value that is the Arithmetic mean of the EBIT

(II) Financial Risk

"Financial Risk is caused by the introduction of debt into the capital structure of a company". The use of debt in the capital structure of a company not only increases the return to the shareholders but also exposes them to the following risks:

1. Increased variability in the shareholders earnings.

2. The threat of insolvency.

1. Consumer goods industries face fluctuations in sales. A company with sales fluctuations cannot employ more debt as the earnings of the shareholders will vary. Even a small percentage change in sales can cause a dramatic change in the earning per share. So shareholders of such companies perceive a high degree of risk.

2. During adverse operating conditions when costs increase, companies with usable sales may suffer from liquidity crisis. It may find it tough to meet its obligations in time.

Measurement of Financial Risk

Financial risk can be measured with the help of the following:

(a) Debt-Equity ratio: This ratio expresses the ratio between the long-term debt and owners funds. Long-term debts include Debenture and Term loans. Equity includes the paid-up share to capital plus reserves and surpluses minus operating losses.

$$\text{Debt-equity ratio} = \frac{\text{Long term debt}}{\text{Net worth / Equity}}$$

(b) Debt-Capital ratio: This ratio expresses the relationship between the long-term debt and the total capital of the company. Total capital includes debt as well as net worth. The formula is stated below:

$$\text{Debt-equity ratio} = \frac{\text{Long term debt}}{\text{Total capital employed}}$$

(c) Interest coverage ratio: This ratio indicates the number of times, the fixed interest payable is covered by the earnings of the company. It is computed by applying the following formula:

$$\text{Interest Coverage} = \frac{\text{EBIT}}{\text{Interest}}$$

This ratio is used to test the firm debt-servicing capacity.

Financial risk is viewed as the probability of a company going insolvent due to its inability to meet interest obligations as and when they fall due. Financial risk unlike business risk is controllable. A company can change its financial risk by changing its capital structure.

(F) Time of Floatation

Financial planning involves the decision regarding the timing of floatation of a company's securities. In order to make capital issue successful, the right time must be determined. The timing is related to the economic conditions prevailing in the country. All economies face a simultaneous change in investment, employment, output and prices. Thee changes recur and are called trade cycle. The four phases of a business cycle are described as follows:

1. Boom

This is a period of high investment, high employment and large volume of output in the economy. The prices rise, there is lot of demand for funds and the rate of interest is very high.

2. Recession

This is a period of slow down or fall in the rate of economic growth. This period is associated with falling levels of investment, rising unemployment and falling prices.

3. Depression

This is a period of severe recession. Economic activities are at their lowest. It is a period of crisis. Many business firms close down, resulting in unemployment. There is gloom everywhere.

4. Recovery

This is a period when the business activity shows signs of recovery, since the piled up stock of the Depression period is completely sold and the businessmen look for funds to produce the basic minimum output. This slowly introduces activity gain.

The best time for floating securities is when business is booming and people are optimistic.

(G) Watered Capital

Watered capital refers to a situation where the promoters of the company have paid an excessive price for the assets than what they are really worth at the time of taking over the business. The excessive price paid over and above the real value of assets, is known as watered capital.

(H) Thin Capitalisation

An arrangement in which a company is incorporated with a small share capital and is financed with a large loan from its parent company (Holding company), usually in order to benefit from tax relief or interest payment on loan.

(I) Option

The right to buy or sell a fixed quantity of a commodity, currency, security etc. at a particular date, at a particular price.

An option to buy is known as a call option and is usually used when there is expectation of rising prices. A put option is an option to sell. A put option is exercised when there is an expectation of falling prices.

(J) Bottom Line

Bottom line is that profit figure which is used for calculation of earnings per share. It draws its name from the fact that net income is the bottom line on an income statement.

(K) Annual General Meeting (AGM)

An annual meeting of the shareholders of a company is called an Annual General Meeting. The gap between one annual general meeting and the next annual general meeting cannot be more than 15 months. Shareholders of the company are given 21 days notice.

The usual business activities transacted in an AGM are:

1. Presentation of the audited accounts
2. The appointment of directors and auditors
3. The recommendation of dividends.

(L) Appropriation

An allocation of the net profits of an organisation in its accounts is called appropriation of profits or just appropriation.

(M) At Par

It is also called par value, face value or nominal value. If market value of a security, exceeds the nominal price, it is said to be above par. One the other hand if the market value falls short of nominal value it is called below par.

(N) Gilt-edged Securities (or Gilt)

A fixed interest bearing security or stock issued by government is called gilt edge security. These are considered to be the safest investments, as government is unlikely to default on principal repayments to the investor.

(O) Coupon

The rate of interest paid by a fixed-interest bond is called coupon.

(P) Agency Conflict

Agency conflict is conflict in the interest of the Directors / Manager of a company and that of the shareholders. It is so called because the Directors are to act in the capacity of agents while managing the affairs of the company. They are to act in the best interest of their principal i.e. shareholders. Welfare of shareholders demand an efficient management of the affairs of the company. But 'Directors' pursuing their personal projects may not give required time and may not put in their efforts to enhance the value of the firm.

(Q) Portfolio

All assets and investments owned by a person or business is called portfolio. It may consists of gold coins, stocks, bonds, real estate and cash.

(R) Liquid Asset

Cash or an asset that is easily convertible into cash, is called liquid asset. For e.g. bank deposits, shares and other marketable securities, accounts receivable etc.

(S) Leverage

The existence of fixed cost in the total cost of a firm is called leverage. Leverage increases the profitability and earnings of the shareholders. There are two types of leverages:

(a) Operating leverage

(b) Financial leverage

Operating leverage occurs when fixed costs is a part of a company's total cost. As sales increase the fixed cost gets spread over a large number of units, thereby reducing the fixed cost per unit. A reduction in the fixed cost per unit causes reduction in the operating cost per unit. This leads to increase in the EBIT (Earning Before Interest and Tax).

Financial leverage occurs when company uses a fixed cost bearing funds in the capital structure of a company. A company might have preference share capital on which fixed rate of dividend is payable and may also use fixed-interest bearing term-loans Debentures and bonds etc. Use of such funds increases the equity earnings because these are less costly funds. After paying the fixed cost on these funds, the excess earnings can be transferred towards the earnings of the shareholders.

(T) Cornering the Market

Cornering the market refers to the purchase of a stock or commodity in such a significant amount that trading in that item is no longer competitive. Cornering the market is illegal.

(U) Capital gain

The income derived from selling an investment for an amount of money greater than its purchase price is called capital gain. The investment sold after being held for more than one year, may give rise to long-term capital gain and if held for less than one year, before sale, the capital gain resulting therefore would be termed as short-term capital gain.

■■■

www.ingramcontent.com/pod-product-compliance
Lightning Source LLC
Chambersburg PA
CBHW080603090426

42735CB00016B/3330